M

W

Christian T

Christian Theology

A Brief Introduction

Gareth Jones

Polity Press

First published in 1999 by Polity Press in association with Blackwell Publishers Ltd.

Editorial office:
Polity Press
65 Bridge Street
Cambridge CB2 1UR, UK

Marketing and production:
Blackwell Publishers Ltd
108 Cowley Road
Oxford OX4 1JF, UK

Published in the USA by
Blackwell Publishers Inc.
Commerce Place
350 Main Street
Malden, MA 02148, USA

ISBN 0-7456-1062-5
ISBN 0-7456-1063-3 (pbk)

A catalogue record for this book is available from the British Library and has been applied for from the Library of Congress.

Typeset in 11 on 13 pt Sabon
by Wearset, Boldon, Tyne and Wear.
Printed in Great Britain by MPG Books, Bodmin, Cornwall.

This book is printed on acid-free paper.

Contents

Introduction: What is Christian theology?

This book is written for all students starting out on a study of Christian theology, at whatever level of higher education. It deals specifically with the question 'How do I study Christian theology?' and considers this question explicitly in terms of theological method, its resources and practices. It is not a historical textbook: such a textbook was recently written by Alister McGrath – his *Christian Theology: An Introduction*. (Students will find this and other recommended reading in the Suggestions for Further Reading.) Rather, it is an introductory guide to an academic discipline, one which requires certain skills and techniques, things which need to be taught and learned: Christian theology (henceforth, simply theology).

It follows, therefore, that this book is not about Jewish theology, or Muslim theology, or the comparative study of religion, or the philosophy of religion, and so on. Here I have concentrated solely upon the mechanics of how Christian discourse about God works in a variety of different situations, the common features which different theologies share, what makes them different, and what resources they possess. It also presupposes that God exists, taking theology at its face value, without asking

questions about the justification of **theism**. Whether God exists
or not, theology can be studied as an academic discipline, involving both theoretical and practical matters. This is the argument I
address in this book.

What then is 'theology'? Some introductions begin by referring
to the origins of this idea in the philosophies of Plato and Aristotle, and then its place in the development of Christianity in the
classical world. As significantly, however, the question is one
which thousands of students throughout the world are constantly
trying to answer, both with the assistance of their teachers, books
and discussion and with their own ideas and thoughts. It is,
moreover, a question which involves many different things, so
that one simple answer will not suffice for the many varied situations and environments in which Christians who want to speak
of God live and work. It is easy to say, of course, that theology is
simply 'talk about God'. But what are the grammar, syntax and
vocabulary of such talk? What form and shape do they take? Is
theology a story, or a series of rational propositions? There is no
one single answer, but there are ways of making the questions
more straightforward.

This is true whatever motives one identifies in those who want
to study the way in which people speak of God: whether to
reflect upon the world's important religions, and how they speak
distinctively of their faith; or whether to concentrate solely upon
one religion, as I will in this book, discussing instead the way in
which people and communities within the same religion nevertheless interpret their beliefs differently. Even before attempting to
define theology more closely, then, every student has the task of
assessing where they want to establish the focus of their enquiry.
This book has been written to help in that process of orientation,
by examining the main issues and questions involved in studying
specifically *Christian* theology.

In addition to this matter of differing human situations and
how they influence one's approaches to theology, there is the
equally problematic fact that God, as all religions agree, cannot
be regarded as an object in the world to be picked up, identified,
evaluated and then set down in an ordered place in time and
space. On the contrary, God is always in some sense *other than*
this world and its inhabitants. This means that students of theo-

logy are confronted by a second major obstacle to their under-standing and definition of the subject: not only do they live in a world which manifests many ingenious ways of speaking of what it believes to be the divine; additionally, that divinity, God, can nowhere be seen and identified *as* God!

Given these particular constraints, all that any introduction to theology can attempt to do is to set out before the student the questions and areas of the subject as its author understands them, having first of all considered the scope and context of what he or she understands the discipline to be. Any such introduction must therefore be genuinely *introductory*: it must lead the student into the area it is to discuss. But students must be prepared to under-take the most important steps of the journey towards greater understanding for themselves. How? By reading, writing, think-ing and discussing.

At this stage in a textbook's introduction the student might start to feel uneasy about the amount of factual information that is looming on the horizon – I have read a lot of textbooks with just such a sense of growing alarm. What I want to say about *this* book, however, is that it is not about knowledge, but rather about understanding, and that understanding is something *every* student of theology – be he or she a first-year undergraduate or a university lecturer – has to acquire by going through a series of straightforward processes. Essentially, what I mean is that we are all in the same situation: there is material to be studied and inter-preted, and interpretation is our main task. This is possible because theology functions according to certain principles, so that, after these principles have been mastered, one can go on and consider more deeply some of the issues and questions gener-ated by the subject.

This is what I want to achieve in this book, and the text has been constructed in such a way that the student is gradually introduced to the areas, questions and disciplines of what theo-logy is. Four Parts, concerned respectively with initial considera-tions (I), resources and responsibilities (II), how theology works (III) and today's questions (IV), address in turn the four qualities which any student of this discipline needs for their work: the ability to think, a knowledge of the discipline's principal compo-nents, the skills to use it, and the openness to apply it to the

world in which one finds oneself. If these four qualities are realized in all aspects of a student's reading, writing, discussion and
reflection, then that student will be able to answer, to their own
satisfaction and in their own judgement, the question, What is
theology?

These four areas will be discussed in detail as the book pro-
gresses; but initially certain parameters can be established which
will guide and shape what follows. The reason for doing this is
quite straightforward: to say something about the presuppositions and arguments with which I approach the study of theology
in this book. What I write here is not prescriptive, but rather
descriptive solely of my own position, and is offered to inform
the reader of the background to this text. If something of my
own denomination is evident in this – I am a liberal Anglican,
with some Catholic leanings and the occasional Orthodox conviction – then I want this to inform the reader solely of the way
in which *I* do theology, not the way in which one *should* do theology. As such, it will be a useful exercise for the student to pick
up on some of the characteristics of my own parameters and
guidelines.

Parameters and guidelines

First, and in keeping with the spirit of openness which generally
characterizes the study of theology in the contemporary world, I
want to acknowledge the genuine, sincere and honourable ways
in which different people, of all religions, speak of God. Be they
Jews, Hindus, Muslims, Sikhs, Buddhists, Baha'is or Christians
(to name only a few of many), people everywhere want to speak
of God (though not everyone: I do not thereby reduce agnostics
and atheists to believers). This is an impulse, therefore, which
characterizes much of what makes people human. But at the
same time, it is something which people do, ultimately, in terms
of their own experience, their own perceptions and understanding of God. Let me be clear once again about the scope of this
book: it is an introduction to *Christian* theology. I ask questions
and offer ways into a discussion, for and by the student, of what
it means to attempt to understand the Christian faith. In Thomas

Aquinas's words in the *Summa Theologiae* (written in the thirteenth century CE), theology is 'holy teaching': it is teaching about the central beliefs of Christianity. This is my first parameter.

Second, however, this does not mean that in what follows the other religions of the world will be either ignored or belittled; for any religion which does that is unworthy of its subject. On the contrary, this book keeps in mind the relationship of Christianity to the other religions of the world (in particular, chapter 10 will have more to say on this). What I want to urge upon all students of theology is a humility and an openness to understanding which readily acknowledge that there are different valid ways of speaking of God, so that to negate even one of them prejudicially is to negate them all. I am not writing for Christian believers, therefore, but for people who want to study Christian theology. There is a difference: this book is not an introduction to **catechism**, but to enquiry. This means that the book should be read not as a blueprint for each and every theological argument, but rather as something more akin to a manual of car maintenance, in which certain procedures are set out as straightforwardly as possible. Actually following those procedures is something we each do for ourselves – which is my second principle.

Third, Christian theology is concerned initially with the belief that God is present in the world and has acted within history in Jesus of Nazareth, as revelation of God's will to be with the world and ultimately to save it and its inhabitants. Of course, such a conviction starts from some very clear presuppositions – **axioms**, or statements which allow of no demonstration, but they are the presuppositions of the Christian faith – and theology must take them seriously.

In this sense theology is about revelation pure and simple, and therefore about Jesus Christ pure and simple, which is why Christology dominates so much theology, and why for the Christian faith talk of God is so often and so completely talk of Jesus Christ. But this is a very Protestant view, and is only one of the ways in which Christians understand God's relationship with the world. There are many theologies which speak of God's presence as being as important as God's revelation – for example, in Roman Catholicism; and there are mystical theologies – for example, in the Orthodox traditions – which say that theology is talk about what God is not, rather than what God is. Saying that theology is about revelation pure and simple, therefore, is a statement which should alert the reader to the presence of some distinctive, a priori assumptions.

Fourth, then, it must be acknowledged that the revelation of God in Jesus Christ, which involves people in many different forms of historical, personal and social reflection, is never solely revelation; it is never simply a matter of seeing and knowing God in all of God's glory. Rather, revelation always necessarily involves its opposite, concealment, so that being aware of the presence of God, in some way, is always simultaneously being aware of the absence of God. This is the **paradox** which lies at the heart of the Christian faith, and which, consequently, should be mirrored in every Christian theology: God is both revealed and concealed in everything which is said and believed about Jesus Christ. So, by definition, Christology cannot be the only way to speak of God's relationship with the world.

Fifth, therefore, theology will always be an inexact science; it will always involve the student in a process of argument and counter-argument, statement and counter-statement, application and withdrawal. I can thus offer a second, tentative definition of theology: it is faith seeking understanding, a conviction which Anselm of Canterbury identified in the eleventh century. Although Anselm understood theology in the context of prayer, we can still understand the methodological significance of his argument even in the contemporary world: theology is an activity, a discipline which involves the student in a process of testing and applying arguments and counter-arguments.

Sixth, and finally, I can say a little more about this expression, faith seeking understanding, which will lead naturally into Part I. For the student of theology, who may or may not be a believing Christian, and who may or may not, ultimately, achieve any great degree of understanding, its most important component is the word 'seeking'; for what any student is involved in, in any discipline, is a journey, a dynamic movement in which they develop their own judgement and reflection in engagement with all of the reading, writing and discussion which they encounter. This may or may not be an 'existential' journey, involving the student's personal development; this does not really matter in the context of studying the discipline. What does matter is that the student is open to where this intellectual journey will take them, so that their task as students should be to become more skilled at understanding and interpreting the questions and issues they encounter along the way.

Developing this analogy, I want to argue that this book presents a map, and only one map amongst others, of the terrain which the student of theology will cover. It is by no means complete; nor is it prescriptive, in the sense that it must be followed at all costs. It allows for various digressions along the way, some of which are clearly signposted, but it is a map which contains a definite key, a distinct list of features which the student, at whatever stage of their journey, can consult to find out where they are. This is how this book should be used: as a guide which provides helpful information, ideas and possibilities, as they tackle this discipline. It is not a blueprint, to be followed scrupulously as the student 'builds' theology from the ground up. That is not how the subject works. If the student always bears this in mind in working through what follows, then he or she will be well on the way towards a deeper understanding of the Christian faith in the contemporary world. This is theology.

PART I
Mapping the Terrain

Maps, with keys and routes and features clearly marked, provide a useful way of thinking about and studying theology, certainly when one first approaches it. Moreover, it is a very flexible way of looking at this particular discipline: it encourages the realization that, just as maps can change and be updated as new and different methods of measuring and representing land and its features become available, so theology can change as its methods alter, and as the situations in which people want and try to speak of God change.

'Mapping the terrain' of theology, then, is not a straightforward task, because it is not simply a question of identifying the same monolithic questions that have been around for thousands of years. On the contrary, when one speaks of the task in this way, one is recognizing that certain key features can and should be noted initially, but that this is very much a preliminary stage. The two chapters of this section make more sense of this claim as they give clearer definition to theology and its terrain.

Chapter 1 considers the question of how one understands the relationship between theology and faith. Everyone recognizes that there is such a relationship in Christianity, but how should it be understood? This chapter raises, therefore, the important issues of theory and practice in theology, how they relate to each other, and to what extent one or the other should be allowed to dominate, particularly in relation to the wealth of beliefs, practices and statements which people all over the world hold and make out of their various religious commitments.

Chapter 2 develops further the understanding of theology in chapter 1 by making six claims about the way in which theology speaks of God. Theology is pluralistic, limited, applied, critical, constructive and imaginative. Of course, these qualities do not constitute a complete list of what theology is; as the Fourth

Gospel claims, if one were to attempt to be exhaustive in this manner, '... the world itself could not contain the books that would be written' (John 21: 25). What I am trying to set forth in chapter 2, instead, is an open and suggestive way of looking at the qualities and abilities which go to make up Christian theology. And I hope that as students progress in their understanding of the subject, they will be able to realize these qualities in their own writing and discussion, as well as discovering other areas where such criteria might be important. This section is, after all, concerned with initial considerations.

In what follows, students are provided with a range of arguments and claims about the way in which theology can and should be understood. All of these arguments and claims are illustrated by examples, some of which are drawn from the Christian tradition, which is now nearly 2,000 years old, others of which will be recognized as of immediate social concern. In all cases, however, the emphasis is upon the gradual development of an understanding of the shape and parameters, the terrain, of theology. It is rather like watching a photograph of a mountain range as it emerges in developing solution: as one waits, the plain white photographic paper is gradually transformed by the shadowy outline of peaks and valleys. Not all of the features of theology will emerge in this section, but those that do will equip the reader with the necessary skills and understanding to proceed further with their study of this discipline.

1

Christian Theology and Christian Faith

- Questions of truth and reason in faith and theology
- The universal possibility of faith
- Definitions of belief, practice, ritual and experience
- Relationship between theology and faith
- Practising theology

It is well to be clear at the beginning about the rubric under which this book approaches the relationship between theology and faith. Theology seeks to understand the Christian faith because it believes it to be true. Its truth is not something which can be demonstrated **empirically**; nor is it something which one can prove corresponds to a supernatural order which exists outside of space and time. On the contrary, Christian truth is confessed, and as such originates in an axiom: that God is present in the world, as was revealed in Jesus Christ. Thereafter the specific theological claims of different traditions, and different communities, can be (and were) tested for their coherence against the original confession of faith in Jesus Christ. But they cannot go beyond that revelation, which is received from God and mediated through Christ, the Bible and ensuing Christian reflection (tradition).

In what follows I will use this initial definition as a starting point for everything I want to say about Christian theology and faith. But the student should remember that, as with any rational discipline, theological arguments must be tested to see if they make sense, and that, consequently, the quality of a theological argument cannot be vouchsafed simply because it refers back to the origin of faith. Certainly, Christian theology begins axiomatically; but this does not mean that there is not good and bad theology. One does not have to be a Christian, then, to *study* theology, because in studying the way in which theology works, one is really studying, as with all things academic, the *quality* of arguments, which can be assessed and understood whether or not one believes them to be true.

1   Faith

What is faith? The introduction began by referring to the origin of theology in the classical tradition which preceded Christianity. Studying theology, however, is by no means something everyone does. On the contrary, it is a very specific discipline, one which cannot be undertaken lightly or even accidentally. Having faith, by contrast, is something open to every individual and community. Indeed, if there is one thing that can be said about the way people think about faith, then it is in terms of its universal possibility; that is, anyone and everyone can have it. In this sense, 'being faithful' is something far more appealing, to most people, and far more immediately intelligible, than 'studying theology'.

Certainly, there are denominational differences as to faith's origin, and these cannot be ignored. For example, Protestantism holds that faith comes from God as a gift, through Jesus Christ alone, and it relies upon a very strong sense of the Word of the Bible to establish this principle. Roman Catholicism, by contrast, whilst agreeing that faith is a gift from God, holds also that faith as grace, the presence of God, can come to the individual in a variety of ways – for example, through the **sacraments**, the Church's traditions and personal religious experience (as well as the Bible, of course). And Orthodox churches like the Greek and Russian have a strong sense of the life of faith lived in the power of the Holy Spirit. Such origins are not mutually exclusive. On the contrary, Christian faith is often a combination of all these beliefs taken together. The important thing is not that faith might originate differently for different people, but rather what they believe and how this affects the way they live their lives.

These very simple claims open for discussion the relationship between theology and faith, about which one needs to find a consensus in order to advance a more specific understanding of theology's qualities (because theology is faith seeking understanding). In this chapter, therefore, I ask the questions: what is faith? What models are there for defining the relationship between theology and faith? And how does one move from faith to theology as something distinct, which can then be studied? In this way I intend to move towards a relational understanding of theology and its operations, from the viewpoint of a clear definition of faith.

At least initially, one can illustrate this subject matter by referring to the New Testament, and one of the stories of how the disciples behaved in the presence of Jesus. Of particular interest here is Peter's confession of faith at Caesarea Philippi (Mark 8: 29), which acts as the pivot around which Mark's Gospel turns. When Peter answers Jesus' question, 'Who do you say that I am?', with the words 'You are the Christ', he is making a theological statement, born of faith – in this case his confession of Jesus' Messiahship. On the basis of the definition of theology as faith seeking understanding, one can say that Peter is here confessing faith and seeking understanding by appropriating a title and then applying it to Jesus. Jesus himself then elaborates upon Peter's remark (see Mark 8: 31), developing the theological argument from Peter's initial position. Both Peter and Jesus therefore show how faith and theology are related to each other.

This appears to be reasonably obvious: faith is something which involves an active element, in Peter's case the confession of Jesus being the Christ. Some of the other aspects of faith, which go towards my preliminary definition, are not, however, quite so simple; and obviously, the example of Mark 8: 29 illustrates solely one dimension of being faithful. What I want to do now, therefore, is elaborate this question of definition more fully, thereby providing sufficient ideas and information to be able to tackle this question successfully on a number of different levels. In order to do this, I will now consider some of the ways in which people appear to be faithful, drawing illustrations from different Christian denominations. These ways are belief, practice, custom, experience. They will be considered separately, though they often merge together in real life. Remember that for Christian belief, practice, custom and experience, the axiom I identified at the beginning of this chapter always holds true: God is present in the world, revealed in Jesus Christ.

1.1   Belief

Returning to Peter's confession at Caesarea Philippi, one can say that belief involves an expression or communication of one's own personal convictions, even if that expression is utterly private, as in silent prayer. For Peter this means confessing a belief about the person of Jesus of Nazareth. But for other people in other times and places the nature of belief may be very different. One might, for example, wish to express the conviction that something divine is communicated via natural events, such as rainbows, or earthquakes, or thunderstorms (Martin Luther believed that he heard God speak in a particularly violent thunderstorm, prior to his first celebration of the Mass). This is a straightforward way of speaking of God's presence in the world, in and through material reality.

By contrast, one's religious belief might centre upon a particular text, such as the Bible or certain parts of it. A good example of the biblical foundation of faith is found in contemporary evangelical movements, which at present are strikingly successful in converting people in Latin America to Protestant Christianity. One might even hold fundamentalist views about the Bible's status, such as the conviction that it is literally true. Such news can be seen in a variety of denominations in contemporary society, particularly in the United States, where such beliefs structure life to a strong degree, often with positive benefits.

Belief obviously colours to a marked extent how one speaks of God, because if theology is faith seeking understanding, then such belief is the motor which drives the quest for meaning. This may be true both of the expression of an individual's belief, or that of a community, because in each the motor is the same: belief drives theology forward, both for the individual and for the church or community. Without it, there is little point in speaking of 'God' at all. The need to express one's faith is something positive, and the need to communicate the Word of God has been the motive force behind many evangelical movements – for example, the missionary movement of the nineteenth century.

All this seems to imply that belief is something which can be separated from the way in which people live their everyday lives, which is clearly untrue: belief must be part of that everyday life if it is to be established in the understanding of reality which most people hold to be normative. But at the same time it is possible to speak in this preliminary manner about the way in which belief functions, because the rationale for speaking here of belief is to emphasize its important relationship to theology. Belief, then, is not theology, because theology involves a certain conceptual distance born of the need to understand and communicate, which belief cannot afford; but the two are intimately related. Though their subject matter – God – is one, faith and theology are related as different stages of articulation.

Belief can be interpreted, therefore, on a number of different levels. For example, one might understand it psychologically, which is common in very devotional forms of worship – for example, in the spirituality of the Ignatian Exercises. Or one might regard it in terms of the communal outbursts typical of Pentecostal churches, inspired by the Holy Spirit. The sheer variety of these different interpretations, however, should not be regarded negatively. Rather, the important thing to appreciate is that this variety is a positive consequence of being human. There are many different ways of being human, after all; and so there are many different ways of expressing belief in God, from immediate and spontaneous shouts of joy, to the sober reflection of systematic theology. Belief is the widest ocean the theologian encounters; but that encounter is endlessly challenging. The risk for the student of theology is to overlook or ignore certain expressions of belief, because of presuppositions concerning what belief's character should be. This is always detrimental to any attempt to study theology successfully.

1.2   *Practice*

Unless it is expressed in particularly vague terms, however, belief cannot be reduced solely to the individual's (or community's) verbal communication of what is believed. On the contrary, such belief, which, one might say, seems to be reduced to the level of interior feelings and their subsequent expression, rightly belongs to the world of the psychology of religion; that is, it is an area of human intellect and research, if understood solely in terms of its own autonomy. To bring out its true significance, belief needs to be interpreted in tandem with its partner, practice, because it is practice which indicates the relevance of belief by demonstrating how it changes the way in which people live. In this respect, practice takes the present definition of faith an important stage further.

An example will illustrate this point clearly enough, particularly as it is one found in a variety of different denominations. A significant amount of time in the communion service is devoted to a celebration by the worshippers of a re-enactment of the Last Supper. The belief inherent in this celebration is clearly articulated in the words of Matthew's Gospel:

> Now as they were eating, Jesus took bread, and blessed, and broke it, and gave it to the disciples and said, 'Take, eat; this is my body.' And he took a cup, and when he had given thanks he gave it to them, saying, 'Drink of it, all of you; for this is my blood of the covenant, which is poured out for many for the forgiveness of sins.' (Matthew 26: 26–8)

The text speaks of the belief or conviction that Jesus' death is a singular event which is, however, of meaning for all, this being what Christians celebrate during the Eucharist.

In itself, though, the belief is by no means the only part of the **liturgy**. Explicit in Jesus' words are two imperatives: 'Take, eat', and 'Drink of it'. There is a clear injunction to do something, to practice, to action or behaviour which will make a material difference in the way one lives one's life. Certainly, the Eucharist is based upon doctrines which are open to different interpretations, and there are questions here of memory and presence which are very important. But on a straightforward level this illustrates the point I want to make. And one can go even further, turning this question of practice into a moral one: one should do certain things on the basis of what one believes. This is fundamental to nearly every religion, and central to practically all Christian denominations. Belief necessitates practice, something agreed by all churches.

There are many other examples which could be cited here to illustrate this understanding of practice and its close relationship with belief, and some of them can be drawn from the same liturgical context, such as prayer, hymnody and the sermon. But the important thing to recognize is that such practice calls the believer to act upon his or her faith by participating in certain elements of service. There is, then, what one might call an act of personal and/or communal identification which occurs when belief becomes practice. Without such action, belief remains passive. And although passivity has a role in, for example, prayer, it cannot be the entire story of faith.

1.3   Custom

One of the most important aspects of practice, consequently, is that it makes a difference, no matter how small, to how one lives one's life; because even if a practice is adopted lightly, it still constitutes a different activity, one in which one might not otherwise engage. Entering or leaving anything, be it a practice or somebody's life, is always significant for someone or something. Faith is a way of life, for Christianity *the* way of life. Therefore one should expect it to influence all of the activities of human existence, however mundane.

There is no sense, therefore, in which practice can be understood simply as empty posturing. Yet this is the accusation which is often levelled at custom, such that 'custom' is defined very negatively. For example, many past commentators criticized unthinkingly the rituals of indigenous populations, regarding them as the charades of a superstitious people. Similarly, people have often ridiculed the way in which people venerate statues and icons, particularly those associated with purportedly miraculous events. These are empty customs, claim such sceptics, and have no place in our understanding of the modern world and the people in it. This negative judgement has become largely prevalent in Western Europe and North America, where industrial societies have historically generated many people familiar and comfortable with the presuppositions of the post-**Enlightenment** world-view.

By contrast, I want to assert an important place for custom in the present understanding of faith and its characteristics, not simply because so many people honourably regard such customs as central to the celebration of their faith, but also because of the symbolic importance of custom itself. Custom stands alongside belief and practice, because it reveals something about the ways in which people attempt to communicate their experience of, or conviction about, God. In this sense, customs symbolize something central to the way in which the vast majority of people live with their faith: namely, the paradoxical feeling of the simultaneous absence and presence of the divine in everyday life.

This is a difficult idea, and needs unpacking. In the Christian tradition, the nearly 2,000 years of history during which people have tried to speak of God in relation to Jesus Christ, there has been a clear distinction between the **apophatic** and the **kataphatic** in theology. Simply, these words can be translated as referring to the absence and presence of God respectively, with the former in particular being very important for many Christian ideas about the mystery of God's being and its revelation. It is the absence of God which most keenly informs the way in which people generally think of customs, because they are ways of symbolizing the mystery which surrounds the God who is not, to all appearances, present in the world.

In this way customs possess great suggestive power. Like art and its images, be they visual, audible or in any other way sensory, such customs seek to take one beyond the everyday world to a different level of understanding. Such customs are thereby intimately related to human imagination, which shapes them and gives them meaning as they are perceived, enacted and understood. An example of this is the extended service of the Orthodox Easter celebration, during which such elements as the reading of the Acts of the Apostles, the episodic though rapid process of the priests through the standing congregation, and the procession around the outside of the church, led again by the priests, evoke the beguiling mystery of God's sacrifice on Golgotha, as it is understood by believers. Indeed, the Orthodox tradition is particularly rich in such symbolic customs, as it is equally rich in a powerful sense of the absent God and the apophatic tradition which attempts to articulate this sense to those who believe.

Custom, therefore, is clearly different from both belief and practice. It is arguably secondary to the former, but in many ways stands alongside the latter as an important expression of what it means to believe in God and to be influenced by that belief in how one lives. Moreover, such customs, in non-verbal form, are very similar to the way in which theologians attempt to speak about God, and it is important to recognize that any such custom, which symbolizes something of the way in which people believe in God, can articulate something fundamental about the perceived relationship between God and humanity: a picture paints a thousand words, as the saying goes, and drawing pictures is central to the customary activity of believers.

1.4   Religious experience

Belief, practice and custom, then: these three are things which people throughout the world, whatever their personal or communal convictions, share in act and expression. But all these can be participated in without the one ingredient which many would argue is so central to faith that without it there is no such thing: namely, religious experience, by which I mean an immediate sensation or intuition of contact with God. I have left it until after the other three have been considered because of its problematic character, but it cannot be ignored.

The entire question of what constitutes experience in general, how it is understood, shared, interpreted and communicated, is an impossible one to answer definitively, although philosophy has been attempting this task for thousands of years, since before Plato and Aristotle, and is arguably still no further towards defining what experience is (but see chapter 3). Recently, such reflection has linked all experience to language, as the basis of every aspect of being human. But even here there are great difficulties, since an absence of language does not mean an absence of experience or communication (and some might want to argue that the absence of language actually enhances one's experience of the world in which one lives). Nevertheless, the fact remains that religious experience, at least in popular perception if nowhere else, remains the primary concern of faith itself, and the principal authority to which many people appeal when they seek to substantiate the claims they want to make for their own beliefs, practices and customs.

Examples of this abound in the Christian tradition: one has only to think of Luther's thunderstorm, or Paul's blindness on the road to Damascus, or Augustine's voice from nowhere, heard in the garden. It is also particularly important in contemporary evangelical churches. Nor is it restricted to Christianity: Judaism abounds in such examples of religious experience, as the stories of the patriarchs and prophets testify. More recently, many denominations have appealed to the primary religious experience of their founders or elders as the authority for the way in which they live their lives. One thinks here of such groups as the Mormons, for whom the visions of Joseph Smith are central, and the spiritualist churches, where divine inspiration grants the recipient special status, at least as long as that inspiration lasts. All these examples, and others, testify to the fact that religious experience is, and always has been, integral to the way in which many people think about faith.

This popular perception is problematic for theology, because the appeal to instant authority, to direct communication with God (particularly the Holy Spirit), short-circuits the reflective, critical and constructive processes by which the theologian works. Indeed, one can go further, stating that the existence of a very strong sense of religious experience in an individual or community generally precludes the existence of a strong theological tradition, because if authority is immediately realizable, in terms of direct experience of God, then who needs theology, with its seemingly painstaking progression towards, at best, imperfect understanding? Pentecostal churches today are not great breeding-grounds for theologians in this academic sense, however profound some of their actions and words may be. Relatedly, the

Roman Catholic and Anglican Churches possess rich theological traditions. But the authority of the ecclesial hierarchies in these Churches is hardly compatible with the experiential authority which one finds in, say, fundamentalist congregations in Britain and the United States.

Certainly, these remarks should not be taken as definitive, and the student is advised to look around and see what is happening in their own world, where people claiming religious experiences are never far away. The point here, however, is that to speak of *religious* experience is doubly problematic: it begs huge questions about how we define 'experience' itself, and it raises the ugly spectre of dictatorship (literally, for many regard religious communications as being 'dictated' to them by God). Thus, although more will be said about language and experience and the way in which they impinge upon the workings of theology, one needs to be very careful in speaking of religious experience. It is notoriously difficult to construct a meaningful theology on the basis of it.

2   The relationship between theology and faith

In seeking to understand this relationship, therefore, one is on safer ground if one concentrates upon belief, practice and custom. Although some theologians, such as Friedrich Schleiermacher, have attempted to construct a theological system on the basis of an analysis of what it is to be religious and to 'sense' or 'feel' God, overwhelmingly it is the way in which ordinary people believe and act, without apparently special visions or insights, which establishes a good theology, one that seeks meaningfully to understand faith in relation to its social context.

In this sense one can make a useful distinction between 'Religion', an idealization which is often turned into a sombre and impressively singular monument, and ordinary, everyday faith, which is mediated by its expression in belief, practice and custom. This distinction, which might appear more confusing than it is, can be illustrated by reference to the theology of Karl Barth, the greatest Protestant theologian of the twentieth century, and one of the theologians with whom every student should wrestle.

In 1919 Karl Barth wrote a justly famous commentary on Paul's Letter to the Romans, provoked by his life and work as a minister in Safenwil, Switzerland. Barth argued that the heart of the Gospel had to be addressed to the way in which people actually lived, rather than in terms of the lofty, nebulous sentiments to which they might aspire, such as **liberalism** and culture (though these might be goals in their own right, they are no substitute for the Word of God, argues Barth). Hence, Barth would endorse the present definition of faith as something positive – an attempt to establish theology in the relationship between a real God and a real people, living real lives in the real world. Because 'Religion' had been turned into an idol in Germany by 1919, however, in Barth's view at least, Barth refused to speak of religion. Rather, he took every opportunity to attack it and its false presumptions, culminating in his notorious 1920–1 lectures on Schleiermacher's theology of feeling. Barth hated 'Religion' and its chief authority, 'religious experience', arguing that it was opposed to theology, which sought no authority for itself but solely the opportunity to reflect upon and then articulate, however imperfectly, an understanding of the true Word of God.

This emphasis upon belief, practice and customs, rather than 'Religion', highlights the most important point which I want to identify here: namely, that theology begins not in general questions, but in a consideration of particular circumstances, their constituents, and what they have to say about the way in which those living in them relate to God. Theology, consequently, is always 'something' theology; it is always qualified by a context, and an adjective, be it social, political, historical or anything else one cares to mention. This, essentially, was Barth's point: his commentary on Romans was to all intents and purposes *Safenwil* theology, which Barth opposed to 'Religion', and which he passionately believed had some significance for other people living in the aftermath of the First World War. Whether Barth was right or wrong does not matter here. What is important for our understanding of the relationship between faith and theology is how Barth qualified what he had to say about God (theology) on the basis of his life and work in his parish (faith).

This is the understanding of the relationship between theology and faith which I want to advance in this chapter. It is not a case of theology replacing faith, or being faithful, or repeating belief and practice in words: each of these accusations, and others, have been incorrectly levelled at the way in which faith and theology relate to each other. Instead, I want to understand the way in which faith always qualifies theology. If it does not, then that 'theology' is not really talk about the God who addresses people in their daily lives, but about 'God', a fitting counterpart to 'Religion'. Theology is not about reified entities. It is about reality, which is inherently messy. And being messy is something good, because it is something natural: a theology which seeks always to smooth away life's rough edges is not likely to be a good theology.

Similarly, of course, good theology always qualifies the ways in which people understand faith, in so far as its belief, practice and customs should be informed and enriched by the critical, constructive work of the theologians who are part of that society and/or community. One is justified, therefore, in speaking of a symbiotic relationship between faith and theology, in which each informs, qualifies and colours the other, to the mutual enrichment of both. We study this by understanding the processes by which theology interprets faith, and faith informs theological reflection. Remember, whether we believe Christianity to be true or not, *methodologically* we study how arguments work.

3   The move from faith to theology

Equipped with this initial understanding of the relationship between faith and theology, and, as important, of what it is not, we can now go on and make some claims about the way in which a person moves from being faithful to doing theology, and what this development means for the student. Here I will map out one or two of the important features of the general landscape which I am trying to cover in this book, features such as the status of theologians, their general standpoint and perspective, and their relationship to the society and community within which they live and work, points which are relevant whatever denomination the theologian represents. These brief reflections will be fleshed out later in the book, particularly in chapters 7 and 8.

First, it is important to acknowledge that being faithful and doing theology are not mutually exclusive. On the contrary, the theologian will be a believer, part of a world of belief, practice and custom. The theologian is 'in' the realm of faith, its power, activities and responsibilities. To ignore this would mean falling into the trap of regarding 'Religion' once again as a monument which one can walk endlessly around, without ever coming to grips with.

Second, however, the theologian is also 'outside' faith, in the sense that he or she must stand back somewhat in order to reflect upon their faith. This is the sense of the claim that theology is second-order reflection: it reflects upon faith as it relates to it. The nature of this relationship is not, of course, one of absolute separation. But it is distinct enough to define the office of the theologian as a separate office in the believing community. Rather like the prophets in Judaism, therefore, the theologians' task is to address what they see happening in their world, and indeed what they believe they *should* see. There is a strong role for corrective description in theological discourse, analogous to the moral emphasis of practice which was identified earlier.

Both 'in' and 'out', therefore, the theologian stands always on the edge of things, on the borderlands, one might say, of faith and society. Like Jeremiah's, it is an uncomfortable position, and one that is dangerously prone to romanticism, an unfortunate tendency which often afflicts theologians as they seek to understand their work. Examples of the better aspects of this office, however, abound in the Christian tradition: one thinks of Paul's travels in the Roman Empire, always on the periphery of society and its institutions; of Augustine of Hippo writing his *City of God*, fearfully aware of the destructive arrival of the barbarians from across the Mediterranean; of Martin Luther in 1521–2, alone in the Wartburg translating the New Testament into German, thereby establishing the modern version of his language; of Karl Barth, writing his commentary on Romans in neutral Switzerland as Europe was at war; and of Martin Luther King's proclamation of the gospel as a challenge to segregation and the denial of human rights to African-Americans. All these individuals, and the communities within which they worked, illustrate the point I want to make here. Every denomination can provide its own examples.

The move from faith to theology and back again, therefore, is always problematic: it involves both reflection and activity, repose and movement, reading and debate, writing and thought, and as these factors gel together, talk of God is constantly informed by the realities of the world and society in which people live and work. The study of theology is equally burdened with these responsibilities, because even if students themselves do not share the beliefs of the theologian or community they are studying, the responsibility to *relate* their ideas to the contemporary situation remains. Studying theology is always relational. It always draws its student into the craft of interpretation. In this way theology is always an *applied* science – applied to the world in which the theologian lives.

Theology, then, shares many qualities with faith; but it possesses others which make it distinct. What I have argued in this chapter is that neither theology nor faith stands alone, that the movement from one to the other is always a partial qualification of any principles or convictions to which one might care, or seek, to give importance. This process of qualification, moreover, never ends. As theology returns to faith, which then in turn returns to self-reflection and so to further theology, one recognizes the Christian tradition which, in nearly 2,000 years, has constantly sought understanding in, by and through faith.

At the same time, theology must be differentiated from faith, just as theology is not the same thing as religious studies; for theology is a discipline which involves certain qualities which help to define its peculiar questions and responsibilities. In the next chapter we consider these qualities, some of which are predictable and to a certain extent familiar, others of which may surprise the student.

2
Christian Theology: Some Important Qualities

- Identification of theology's character, initially via discussion of relationship with authority
- Definition of theology in terms of its practical qualities:
  - pluralistic
  - limited
  - applied
  - critical
  - constructive
  - imaginative
- Relation of these methodological qualities to the resources and responsibilities of theology

The points made in the first chapter boil down to a question about the theologian's attitude, and that of the student of theology, namely: how do they approach the subject? To a great extent this is true of all academic disciplines, as it is also true of people working in other professions. But at the same time it is peculiarly distinctive of theology to demand a *specific* attitude of its practitioners, at whatever level. This necessary attitude for the student of theology is characterized by an understanding that absolute answers and definitions, such as 'Religion', 'Belief', 'Theology', are impossible (and undesirable) to obtain, and that instead, what is called for is an acceptance that it is overwhelmingly concerned with something that cannot be identified, measured and communicated with any precision. Karl Barth once said:

'When the angels read my theology, they will laugh.' The attitude Barth was alluding to is *humility*.

In this context humility is not that psychological conditioning which sometimes leads to insecurity and doubt and many of their damaging implications. Rather, it is acceptance of the fact that the subject being studied cannot identify and advance any absolute information or knowledge which can be regarded as normative, thereby being used to regulate how people think about certain problems, ideas and persons. Theology should not attempt to claim any special access to knowledge or understanding which raises it above the level of ordinary talk about God. Theologians are not, nor can they be, gnostics, people who claim a unique relationship with God on the basis of what they believe is 'within' them. Theologians are ordinary people, where by 'ordinary' I mean that they have the same potential resources as anyone else who wants to speak of God. A Roman Catholic theologian who teaches at a university starts out from the same place as a lay Roman Catholic theologian; and the same holds true for other denominations.

Why should theologians adopt this humble attitude towards their discipline? Because the alternative – certainty – leads to arrogance and closure, an unwillingness to listen to other viewpoints and voices, the conviction that there is only one right way to speak of God. In theological method, such certainty is often accompanied by reductionism and positivism, principles which argue that theology must be established upon certain irreducible facts, which in turn can be identified in the history and texts of Christianity if one looks hard enough.

More specifically, reductionism is the tendency to think in terms of simple absolutes, notions which are meaningful only if one adopts a very monolithic attitude towards the variety of ways in which people believe and articulate their faith. A very good example of reductionist tendencies, identified in the last chapter, is the conviction that 'Religion' is identifiably a single entity, which one can package, label and display for understanding and edification. But one cannot do this; and if one tries, one is guilty of insensitivity towards the origin of any talk about God – its specific context. This is true for Jew, Christian and Muslim alike, and equally true for those of different Christian denominations.

Positivism is a related theological vice, which claims that it is possible to gain objective knowledge and information about ideas, persons and events by applying to them certain criteria of judgement, which then produce 'measurements' which can be relied upon with confidence. In theology an example of positivism can be found in fundamentalism, particularly its claim that the literal, objective meaning of the Bible is identifiable, and therefore binding upon the way in which people, in any situation, read biblical texts. Fundamentalism asserts a single meaning of the Bible, 'lifting it out' of the texts therein rather as one would fillet a fish (the leftovers being equally useless). The confidence with which this action is undertaken is often positivistic; its results are inherently reductionist, identifying 'The Meaning of the Bible' in a way which leaves no room for discussion or debate, or for the process of seeking understanding. Of course, there are many examples of good evangelical biblical theologies, where people attempt to speak of 'the meaning of the Bible' as constructively as possible. But they do so whilst recognizing the methodological constraints under which they operate. As has already been emphasized strongly, theology requires a degree of flexibility which positivism and reductionism simply rule out.

The root cause of the turn towards reductionism and positivism is a natural human desire for clear, absolute authority, which goes by different names ('reason', 'Church', 'Spirit', 'Bible') but which in the modern era has been most often associated with a particular understanding of the workings of the natural sciences, their ability to provide empirically verifiable results and their reliability as the basis of a way of life. By contrast, theological humility cannot appeal to such ability and reliability. It cannot claim to have empirically verifiable foundations, because it denies the claim that God and God's revelation are in any way empirically verifiable. Instead, humility argues that the authority which the theologian seeks can be found only in the meaning of their ways of speaking of God, be it explicitly biblical or inherently traditional. It cannot be an absolute authority. It exists solely in the degree to which a particular theology is helpful to people in their attempt to understand faith. The theologian's true authority, therefore, is always practical, because practical authority relates theology to people and to God.

A very good recent example illustrating this argument was the debate surrounding the ordination of women to the priesthood in the Church of England. The different sides of that debate appealed variously to the authorities of Bible and tradition, and put forward arguments to support their views. Ultimately, however, no absolute, certain answer to the question could be identified and subsequently used to settle all ecclesial disagreements. Instead, the argument fell back upon a deeper, more practical question: how can we speak of there being one people of God, when we divide that people into two sexes, male and female? The argument for unity carried the day, because it best reflected the practical need of theology, to address the way in which people actually live their daily lives: as people together, not divided.

To develop this idea further, I will now discuss six qualities which a theology should humbly seek to embody. The list is not closed, and students are encouraged to think and read around this subject to discover a feel for the way in which any theology forms itself around all, some or none of these things. As always, I am writing here cross-denominationally; but differences are as significant as similarities. The important thing is to think of these not as 'packets' of information or knowledge which must be included in every argument or essay, but rather as qualities which should inform the way in which one approaches the business of speaking theologically. They characterize preferred behaviour, rather than an objective state of affairs.

1   Theology is pluralistic

The opposite of 'absolute', in the theological context as elsewhere, is 'relative', which means that an idea, person or event is related to the specific circumstances in which it occurs, as well as to other ideas, persons and events. In contemporary theology this idea is called **pluralism**, something which has received enormous coverage and commentary over the last twenty-five years, and which promises to dominate much theological discussion for the foreseeable future. To call theology 'pluralistic' is to say that there are different ways of speaking of God, and therefore of seeking to understand faith. Though faith may be singular, theology is pluralistic, because it recognizes that the different circumstances in which people speak about God will naturally lead to different statements. Today the term for this tendency is 'contextual theology', which again is a dominant motif in contemporary discussion.

This is a very important point, because it serves as protection against the twin dangers of reductionism and positivism. It is, moreover, strongly established in common sense. It stands to reason, for example, that a Roman Catholic priest living in El Salvador, a Presbyterian minister living in Charlotte, North Carolina, and an Anglican priest living in north Oxfordshire, will say different things about God because of the entirely different worlds in which they live and within which they must communicate with their fellow believers. Certainly, they may agree on the fundamentals of what it is to believe in God as Christians. But the language and vocabularies they employ to make that communication will be very different.

This emphasis upon theological pluralism has resulted in a series of different contextual theologies, such as liberation theology (South and Central America), political theology (Europe), black theology (Africa and USA), feminist theology (USA), womanist theology (USA), coconut theology (the Pacific), banana theology (the Caribbean), water-buffalo theology (South-East Asia). The odd names should not fool anyone; what theologians are attempting to do here is to relate their talk about God to the specific circumstances of the society in which they live. The authority they seek is established practically in the lived experience of the audience they wish to address, and in the God who comes to those same people. Their theologies are contextual: they arise from, and communicate to, specific communities in specific situations. This is a model for the way in which theology should function.

2   Theology is limited

Theology is pluralistic, therefore, which means that there are as many different ways of speaking about God as there are faith contexts. But this does not mean that 'anything goes'. One can still be theologically *wrong*; one can still say things which are contrary to Christian faith. A clear example of this was the claim made by the South African Reformed Church in the 1930s that the gospel of Jesus Christ supported and even advocated apartheid. Sometimes, as in this case, it is necessary to stand up and oppose what people want to say about God; to argue that their understanding of the Christian faith is misguided, and in need of change. This is one of the central tasks of theology and theological argument. And it is a task which is still vital today. Theologians, like other figures in society, must stand up and argue that certain behaviour, be it towards Bosnian Muslims or Palestinians or workers in abortion clinics in the United States, is straightforwardly wrong.

To develop this point more fully, I want to use the word 'limited', in the sense of 'rooted' or 'established', and argue that each and every theology comes with certain parameters and limits simply because of the context or situation in which it is articulated. Being limited, therefore, is a result of being pluralistic: both terms point towards every theology's existence in a particular social, cultural, political and economic world, something which governs what the theologian can and should say. In this sense, one does not judge a theology adversely because it does not agree with what one might, in one's own situation, say about God. One judges a theology – like that of the South African Reformed Church in the 1930s – on the basis of the responsibilities it undertakes or ignores. A theology, consequently, cannot simply be tested against the perceived authority of such monolithic entities as the 'Church' or the 'Bible'. Rather, it must be tested against the situation in which it is articulated and which it seeks to address.

An excellent example of a theologian who takes this argument seriously is Stanley Hauerwas, a Methodist who teaches at the Divinity School of Duke University, North Carolina. One of Hauerwas's most recent collection of essays, *Dispatches from the Front*, contains a sequence of pieces on pacifism and whether it is possible in any situation for Christians to go to war. Hauerwas explicitly relates his arguments to the military policies of the United States government, particularly with reference to the Gulf

War in 1991. That Hauerwas opposed that war, for a variety of reasons (theological and non-theological), is not the key issue here, which is rather that the theologian is duty-bound to address the issues which his own situation generates. In the United States, Hauerwas perceived that an overtly militaristic foreign policy in the early 1990s pulled the country into immorality – and, as a theologian, he therefore said so quite straightforwardly. This is a good model for the student of theology to adopt, because this sense of limiting theology makes theology relevant.

Limiting theology in this way is an excellent and necessary check upon the activities of theologians, and it is one of the best ways in which students can learn about the operations of the discipline. The key principle here is testing, and it is something which can be carried out – indeed, which should be carried out – every time one opens a book of theology. The question to be asked of any such book arises naturally out of theology's definition as faith seeking understanding: how does one's understanding function in the world of one's faith? The question works by returning theology's theoretical discussion to the world in which it originated, and to the practical circumstances which it must address. A theology which does not, or cannot, do this is a bad theology – not because it fails to measure up to someone's prejudices and presuppositions, but because it remains speculative rather than directed towards situations in which people need help in understanding what and how they believe.

3   Theology is applied

All this is a way of saying that good theology is applied: it is focused upon, and directed towards, a specific context and the people who live within that context. An example of this is coconut theology, which originates in the Pacific islands, and which uses the single most important commodity of those islands, the coconut and its products, to articulate its understanding of the Christian faith and God's relationship with the world. How does it do this? By relating the aspects of the coconut to Christian doctrine. Thus, the 'face' of the coconut reflects the humanity of Christ; the partition of the shell into three parts, the

Trinity; the flesh and milk of the coconut, the body and blood of Christ; the shell itself, the cup of sharing. This is theological interpretation applied to a dominant social **metaphor** of the Pacific region. All the contextual theologies identified above do the same thing, though with different 'props'; for the aim of the theologian is to communicate meaning and understanding to their own society. This is as true for a conservative, traditional theologian discussing the theology of the sacraments in a Roman Catholic seminary in North America as it is for the most progressive contextual theologian living on a South Seas island.

If I argue, then, that theology is broadly theoretical, but that theory in my sense is inherently practical and not to be confused with abstraction, what do I mean? Many people would argue that this is simply obtuse, that theory is indeed abstraction, and that abstracting away from the particulars of a social context is a bad thing. This is not what theory means, however, even though bad theoreticians may conduct themselves in this way. 'Theory' is in fact 'looking at': *theoria*, the Greek root of the English word, carries this meaning quite forcibly. And by looking at something, and turning it around and around for inspection from different angles, one can move towards an understanding of that thing, be it a problem or an idea or an event or an object. The instinct to be theoretical is entirely natural: witness the way a baby, when given a new toy, will turn it round and round, almost in wonder, until it has a clear picture of what it thinks the present is (which might of course be very different from what the present was intended to be!). Then the child is off, playing with the toy, or possibly rejecting it in disgust or boredom; both are practical responses to the moments of theoretical reflection.

What this means is that theory is the necessary precursor to practice: that it is something – 'looking' – we all do before we proceed towards effecting a specific understanding of what we think we see in our social context. This is why I have identified as a distinctive quality of theology its application: because I want to emphasize the dynamic element involved in moving from theory to practice, from looking to doing. It is not, after all, something which occurs simply when theory and practice collapse into one another, as some theologians like to argue. People are still human; they still look before they act, unless they claim to be entirely instinctive and non-reflective (which is itself a reflective claim). Incorporating this fact into one's understanding and definition of theology, therefore, is a way of acknowledging one of the central qualities of being human. It makes theology a recognizable discipline, something people see and do theoretically and practically.

Socially, this theoretical stage is often best recognized (at least it should be) in the workings of democracy, where people acknowledge and listen to various points of view (looking) before coming to a conclusion which they then go on to act upon (hopefully). Examples of this would be the televised debates between presidential candidates in the United States, for example, Reagan–Carter or Bush–Dukakis or Bush–Clinton, which since the 1980s have become increasingly important in influencing the way in which voters perceive the candidates (and which now have echoes in the United Kingdom). Democracy clearly illustrates the necessity of having moments of reflection within the apparently practical decision-making process. When this happens, societies elect responsive governments which listen to the people and attempt to explain and justify their policies, which are tested within that same society. When it does not happen, however, societies elect governments according to set presuppositions and prejudices, as has too frequently occurred in post-war British politics. The results of such a theoretical failure are evident practically in the crises facing so many areas of British society and government in the 1990s.

Each of the qualities described by these adjectives – pluralistic, limited, applied – refer to the context in which the theologian lives and works, and are concerned with the comportment with which he or she approaches the task of communicating directly with other people and groups. At the same time, however, every theologian must demonstrate certain 'inward' qualities, ones which form and regulate beneficially the style and methods by which he or she seeks to articulate and communicate understanding and meaning. Such qualities are inherently self-regulating: instigating them evokes in the theologian's activity standards which have integrity simply for their own sake. At the same time, such qualities turn the theologian away from a concern solely with human interests, towards that which is beyond even in the midst of life: God. I now want to turn to three of these qualities, elaborating at some length what I mean by the above comments.

4   Theology is critical

'Critical', at least in popular usage, is generally taken to mean something negative and judgemental. If, for example, the leader of Her Majesty's Opposition in Britain criticizes the Prime Minister, or if in the United States a Republican Congressman attacks a Democratic President, then one can take it for granted that, nine times out of ten, they are not being constructive. In theology, however, as in any form of reflection, 'critical' has a very different meaning. In theology, being critical means being reasoned, thoughtful and consistent. In previous times, it was usual and respected to speak of 'systematic theology', where 'systematic' meant just such a reasoned, thoughtful and consistent expression of one's understanding of the central beliefs of the Christian faith. Today systematic theology tends to be regarded as anachronistic, as belonging to an era when theologians like Karl Barth and Hans Urs von Balthasar wrote huge volumes with titles like *Church Dogmatics* and *The Glory of the Lord*, the sheer generality of which prefigures the massiveness of the texts themselves. People do not, on the whole, like huge books, and students in the 1990s have grown not to like systematic theology, which they regard as somehow unnatural. Better by far to apply theology to very practical goals, they argue.

Certainly there was a tendency for systematic theologies to attempt to be absolutely relevant and omniscient, which led inevitably to reductionist and positivist tendencies. But this does not mean that the attributes of reasonableness, thoughtfulness and consistency are no longer relevant. On the contrary, the aspirations of any decent systematic theology to be critical in this sense are entirely relevant to the process by which a theology seeks to be pluralistic, limited and applied. Being critical is simply the other side of the coin. It is a question of both/and, rather than either/or: being critical qualifies being contextual, and vice versa. A good example of this is Avery Dulles's book *The Craft of Theology*. Dulles is a conservative American Roman Catholic theologian, who writes about traditional doctrinal questions such as the Church and the personhood of Christ. But in writing crit-ical systematic theology, Dulles also demonstrates that the *craft* of theology, as a learned skill, is by necessity something limited and applied. The craft metaphor is very important, because just as one practises carpentry to become better at it, so one practises theology.

Moreover, being critical is a necessary human attribute, a skill, which must be developed by individuals and communities as they seek to understand and communicate that understanding in their own societies. In this respect, being critical is the development of being playful which one recognizes in children, which I discussed above. As a child, one playfully rolls a present around and around, working out what it might be and what it might be used for. As an adult, one playfully rolls around ideas and problems, considering them from different angles and perspectives, in order to arrive at a considered understanding of their meaning and sig-nificance. Jesus' parables in the New Testament work this way, as he teaches people the meaning of the Kingdom of God – a point important for contemporary evangelical theologies.

Being critical, then, is part of the ongoing process of being human; but it is a recognizably distinct stage of that process. In this sense, all theologians should be critical, because all theolo-gians should be human, and should thereby demonstrate all the playful attributes which humans bring to their attempts to under-stand their lives and relationships, including in many cases that with God. Being critical for a theologian, consequently, means being reasonable, thoughtful and consistent, at the same time as being pluralistic, limited and applied. It means being a skilled theologian, where the skills in question are not an esoteric wisdom handed down secretly from generation to generation, but rather the simple constituents of being human and wishing to communicate with others. These qualities are necessary whatever context one lives in – North, South, East or West. They define the linguistic character of human life, individually and socially. They also constitute the primary reason for continuing in higher educa-tion – something which studying theology illustrates as well as studying any other of the humanities.

5   Theology is constructive

At the same time as being critical, however, theology must also be constructive; that is, it should go beyond the requirements of being reasonable, thoughtful and consistent, towards being provocative, engaging and demanding. Theology must be constructive by turning debate and discussion towards the quest for solutions; for it is solutions, or goals, which theology ultimately seeks to articulate. Humility may well be the theologian's principal attitude; nevertheless, there must be no shying away from the attempt to say how one understands God's relationship with the world, on the basis of one's individual and communal faith.

One of the most obvious examples of this process can be found in the very earliest years and texts of Christianity, when the conviction of believers that the end of the world was about to arrive with the inauguration of the Kingdom of God and the coming in glory of the Son of Man, dominated the way in which belief and practice were understood within the Jewish society of the time. The conviction that the end of the world was about to occur thus manifested itself in a very constructive fashion, which can be recognized in Paul's letters to his various churches, in which many urgent social and cultural questions are addressed theologically.

'Constructive' does not mean, therefore, building a monumental system or community, within which theologians sit around discussing God and other related issues. Rather, being constructive means addressing the tasks and responsibilities of theology, particularly its contextual application, by directing the individual and community towards recognizably Christian goals. Hence being constructive often means being ethical, where theological ethics is the constructive practice of elaborating what faith seeking understanding means for the lives of people lived *towards* God.

This is a very important point, because construction is a powerful process, in so far as it generates new structures in society and reshapes existing perceptions and attitudes. Linked to the other tasks and responsibilities which have been discussed in this chapter, one can say that being constructive is not simply a matter of being positive; it is also a matter of attempting to take charge of a certain measure of power. In this sense the constructive task of theology, which revolves around the business of building models of how believers may speak of God, is powerful in so far as it offers real, practical alternatives to the way in which people currently live their lives.

Certain key events can be drawn from recent world history to illustrate this point. Martin Luther King, the black civil rights leader murdered in April 1968, is not commonly regarded as a theologian. But his writings, and even more so his speeches, speak in immensely powerful ways of the identity of human and divine goals, and make strong theological claims. For example, Martin Luther King's most famous statement, 'I have a dream', is one of the most powerful rallying cries of constructive social intent made in the last thirty years, and in King's Memphis speech shortly before his assassination was linked implicitly to the theological motif of Moses' seeing the promised land. Similarly, the black activist Steven Biko, who was murdered whilst in South African police custody in 1977, spoke movingly and eloquently of the constructive power of the vision of democracy for all South Africans, a message of social force which led directly to his own death. Since 1977, figures such as Archbishop Desmond Tutu and the Reverend Alan Boesak, as well as the Dominican theologian Albert Nolan, have helped to keep alive Biko's constructive message by giving it explicit theological content, a situation which continues in the new South Africa with the Truth and Reconciliation Commission.

In short, theology's being constructive drags debate beyond the sometimes arid constraints of its responsibility to be both theoretical and practical. It asks, 'Why this way? Towards which goal?' And it expects a clear answer, because sometimes it is the theologian's duty to articulate solely one goal, without being impartial, fair and balanced. If there is a role in theology for inconsistency, therefore, it is when the necessity of a certain message or argument is so strong that the only constructive way forward is to emphasize it at the expense of other factors. The German theologian Dietrich Bonhoeffer came to this conclusion in 1944 when he participated in the 'necessary evil' of the bomb plot to kill Hitler. And he paid for that constructive decision with his life, being murdered by the Gestapo on 9 April 1945.

6   Theology is imaginative

Bonhoeffer imagined a situation in which evil could be removed by a single act, which in turn would facilitate the recovery of the more applied, constructive responsibilities of faith and theology towards the will of God. Bonhoeffer's imagination proved deadly, as did Martin Luther King's and Steven Biko's. But their deaths, however tragic for all of us socially, also marked the triumph of their vision. In death, constructive theology comes face to face with the fate which awaits all goals and aspirations, and which only the imagination, at least in human terms, can overcome. We return, thus, to an issue raised in the first chapter: namely, the question of the apparent absence of God from the world, and the task and responsibility of theology to interpret this absence consistently with its other tasks and responsibilities.

This integral relationship between the apparent absence of God and the role of the theological imagination is so important that one is tempted to identify it as the key link between all theology and faith as the seat of everything we as human beings might ever be able to say, feel or otherwise experience and communicate about God. It was the imagination which Samuel Taylor Coleridge identified as the highest form of human understanding, in his *Biographia Literaria* of 1815. And it is the imagination which exists as the ultimate court of appeal when one wants to say something about the personal God who cannot be directly experienced or identified – a point illustrated by the hymns and prayers of many different Christian denominations.

But how does the imagination work? One could spend hundreds of pages addressing this question, and still not do so adequately. Yet in short one can assert that the imagination works by suggestion, by using images, linguistic or otherwise, to convey an understanding of something which is taken to be inexpressible. Essentially it is the theological imagination which one must rely upon to communicate something of the mystery of God's reality. Without imagination, mystery remains obscurity; with imagination, mystery conveys something of the meaning of the absent and present God. Using imagination, then, theology can address the other five tasks and responsibilities which have been discussed in this chapter. It is one of the clearest demonstrations of humility: the willingness to think beyond the limits of one's own material world.

In this sense imagination is the culminating requirement of theology, the presence of which makes theology meaningful and effective. Without imagination, any theology is reduced to the level of gathering information which, although a useful and honourable task in its own right, is not conducive to articulating humanity's thoughts and feelings about the divine. God, by definition, is not a piece of material, not an object, about which one can gather information. On the contrary, the personal nature of God means that the direct route of information gathering is closed to the theologian. Instead, the theologian must speak by analogy, reasoning from approximately parallel cases. He or she must use specially designed 'tools' to construct models which convey something of the range of feeling and experience to which language can only approximate. Theologians use analogy to say something meaningful about the thousands of metaphors, similes and allusions which human language generates as part of its ever-expanding application to the way in which people live their lives. A good example of this is Sallie McFague's book, *The Body of God*, in which she uses the analogy of the body to speak of God's character and presence in the world, and to make some important points about humanity's responsibility for the environmental well-being of the planet.

As I will demonstrate, this business of relating analogy and metaphor is central to the way in which theologians handle the building blocks of faith seeking understanding – language and experience, the Bible, history and tradition, and society and culture. And as I will also show, this entire process of working through analogy and metaphor, of writing about and discussing the ideas and beliefs which Christianity has of God, is central to the task of applying faith convictions to the world at large. Nothing in theology is truly isolated from other components of the discipline. On the contrary, theology survives because of its ability to relate one thing to another, be it history to social context, the Bible to doctrine, or personal experience to the glories of the Christian tradition. Not to do so would be to turn the claims of faith into monuments of a past civilization. If nothing else, Christianity is about today and tomorrow, not just about what happened 2,000 years ago: the most ardent Roman Catholic traditionalist has in common with the most insistent evangelical a belief in the future of God.

The six qualities considered in this chapter, consequently, all pertain to the methodology of any good theology. They are qualities relevant to the attitude and approach of the theologian, and one can speak with confidence of their consistent presence in a vast array of both past and present theologies, be they those of Augustine in the fifth century or Thomas Aquinas in the thirteenth, or Luther and Calvin in the sixteenth, or Leonardo Boff and Desmond Tutu today. What we have in this chapter, then, is a series of general qualities which have been identified as the requirements of anyone who would speak about God within Christianity, or who would study the way in which others address this matter.

Later on, in Parts II and III, more specific issues will be raised. For example, chapter 4 will look at questions of biblical exegesis, and chapter 5 will consider doctrines such as those of the Trinity and the sacraments. With these examples (and others), students will be intimately involved in a process of testing, application and interpretation, in which these six qualities should be apparent. In this respect it is legitimate to speak of these qualities forming the irreducible, methodological core of studying, and doing, theology. They are what make theology *theology* and, correctly understood, what give theology its extraordinary richness and variety.

What now follows, Part II, will progress naturally through four of the major areas, the building blocks, with which theology has to deal: language and experience, the Bible, history and tradition, and society and culture. As in Part I, no attempt will be made to present an exhaustive analysis. Rather, and in keeping with my metaphor of a map, what I am here concerned to provide is a guide to the terrain: it is for students themselves to pick up the map and judge its relative accuracy, inclusiveness and value. And again, as in Part I, students are expected to provide a good deal of their own application to the words which follow.

- Theology is critical, because it works with rational arguments.
- But theology is also constructive and imaginative, because its object, belief in God, cannot be objectified and hence described.
- Thus there is a plurality of theologies in the world, all limited by and applied to their specific contexts.
- Theology is therefore a subtle and inexact science: it must approach its tasks and responsibilities with sensitivity and openness, not prejudice and presumptions.

PART II

Handling the Building Blocks

Having mapped the terrain of theology, at least methodologically, we now go on to identify the major features which one finds in this territory. I call these 'building blocks', meaning that they are fundamental to the construction of a wide range of theological models, ways in which people speak of God. In Christian theology, the four central building blocks are language and experience, the Bible, history and tradition, and society and culture.

The next four chapters are intended primarily to provide readers with information, ideas and questions about the most important material with which Christian theology operates. At the same time, it would be wrong to imply that these four areas can simply be 'cut out of stone', as one might cut blocks of granite in order to erect a monument to a famous person or event. Things like language and experience, and culture and society, cannot be treated in this fashion. They cannot be treated as if they have sharp, clear edges, beyond which they do not exist or function. Rather, they must be treated with sensitivity and care, always paying attention to their qualities.

This is why I speak of handling these building blocks in the context of theology's questions and responsibilities. For at heart what I really want to say is that theology must be responsible to language and experience, the Bible, history and tradition, and society and culture; that theology must ask, and answer, questions about these things in order to be a functioning discipline, able to communicate its meaning and beliefs to its social context. Handling the building blocks, therefore, is fundamental to good theology, and consequently a necessary part of studying this subject.

3

Language and Experience

- Examination of initial resources of theology as a reflective discipline: language and experience
- Definition of language and experience, addressing questions about:
  their principal characteristics
  the possibility of specifically faithful language and experience
- Relation of theology's qualities, as discussed in chapter 2, to the wider picture of language and experience as theology's initial resources

In what follows I will be looking at how one goes about defining language and experience, how they might be construed as being faithful, and then how they relate, as building blocks, to the theological methods and practices which I discussed in Part I. At the end of this chapter, the student should be ready to go on to tackle the more specifically Christian questions of how one understands the Bible, tradition and history. But initially, here in chapter 3, it is the more general questions of language and experience which are of concern.

1   What is language?

Most people, if asked, would feel fairly safe answering this question. They would quite reasonably argue that language is a vehicle for communication, because one uses it to convey to others particular meanings, names, intentions and so on. If pressed further, they would probably say that language is made up of words and sentences, most of which are broadly descriptive or propositional, communicating information about the apparent state of things, events and plans. If pressed yet further, they would be able to give good examples of this communication process in action: a common one might be a visit to a shopping mall, where language fulfils a clearly useful role in conveying information about price, origin, sell-by-dates, and commodities, enabling customer and cashier to facilitate the purchase of goods and flow of money from wallet to till. In this example there is a strong emphasis upon *using* language in order to convey clear intentions from one group of people, those buying, to another group of people, those selling (and vice versa). This is typical of what many people understand by language.

Some of those questioned, however, might offer a very different understanding of language and how it works. Pointing to such media as film, drama and literature, they might argue that language can be defined as something which cannot convey verbally many of the meanings and ideas which people want to communicate, and that there are other kinds of language. They might cite such things as *body language*, referring to, say, a dance movie with Fred Astaire and Ginger Rogers or, more recently, *Saturday Night Fever* or *Dirty Dancing*. Or they might speak of *musical language*, giving examples from the classical/romantic – Beethoven's Fifth Symphony – or modern – Madonna's *Erotica* – periods. Or they might refer to *written language*, where an author attempts to convey a particular mood or image by building up layer upon layer of descriptive text. Excellent examples of this would be Marcel Proust's *Remembrance of Things Past* and James Joyce's *Ulysses*. Finally, someone might even cite the *private language* of the painter or sculptor – for example, van Gogh or the later work of Marc Chagall – where communication with others is precisely not what concerns the painter.

The tension here seems to be between the majority of people, who want to speak of language as a tool which can be used with precision and effectiveness, and a small minority, who might accept this definition, but who would also want to speak of more mysterious forms of human language. One can summarize this tension as being between those who regard language as *complete*

– fully equipped for its intended purpose of communication – and those who regard it as *incomplete* – really rather inadequate for conveying the breadth and enormity of meaning and intent which people want to pass on to others. There is not necessarily an absolute division between these two admittedly different ways of considering language. But the fact that they are different should not be overlooked. It is not an easy thing to arrive at one satisfactory definition of 'language'.

In fact, one might say that it is *impossible* to arrive at one such definition. Instead, we have to accept that language works in many different ways, only a few of which, in differing circumstances and to varied extents, we have any control over. Language thus has *power*; it can do things which one might not expect, and which one might not desire. An example might be the headline of a newspaper printed in early May 1997, the day after the British general election: 'Blair Beats Major.' Certainly, we *expect* people to realize that this is intended to mean that Tony Blair defeated John Major to become Prime Minister. But we should not be *that* surprised if someone somewhere, however momentarily, thought that Blair had hit Major. In some ways, this is a fanciful illustration of an important point. But it does convey something of the complexities of any attempt to define language and the ways in which it works.

The important point here is that it is impossible to speak of language as if it were a very big, very obvious object which one can easily measure, describe and use, because, on the contrary, language does many different things simultaneously. At no time is it simply one single thing; always it achieves or fails to achieve a wide variety of different ends and goals. Because of this, both theology and philosophy have difficulty in speaking of language ideally, as if there were a formal definition of language which fits each and every situation. Although various schools of thought have attempted to isolate language away from such factors as society, culture, politics and the economic situation, no one has ever succeeded in giving a single definition of language which satisfies the wide range of contexts in which people encounter it in their everyday lives.

This of course is no bad thing; it means that there is always going to be something incomplete about language, something which manifests itself philosophically as language's metaphorical quality, its ability to create images which communicate meaning and intent with varying degrees of subtlety and sophistication. In theology this metaphorical quality finds expression in the idea of *mystery* – the inability of human language to speak adequately of divine reality, which, ultimately, helps to establish the two principles of theology's being pluralistic and limited. Part III will consider the implications of this understanding of mystery for the workings of Christian theology; but here one example will suffice by way of illustration. It comes from the world of the New Testament, which to those who lived in it was an extremely mysterious place, inhabited by demons and spirits. But the New Testament also contains some references to mystery which are more straightforwardly intelligible theologically to people today.

In the New Testament, particularly in Mark's Gospel, many of Jesus' parables function as metaphorical sayings which point towards a reality which cannot be objectively described: namely, the Kingdom of God. These parables, moreover, are often misunderstood by Jesus' audience. They do not succeed in making crystal clear the meaning and intent which Jesus is trying to communicate, but rather approximate that meaning and intent – the Kingdom of God and God's will to save – by drawing upon the experiences of Jesus' listeners and employing everyday imagery. The theme of the Kingdom is central to the first half of Mark's Gospel, where a heightened sense of mystery, driven by the inability of language to convey the heart of Jesus' message and destiny, creates an otherworldly atmosphere, only subsequently penetrated by the strong confession of Peter at Caesarea Philippi (Mark 8: 29). Jesus drives out demons and spirits in the power of the Kingdom. And the motivation for these expulsions is clear and intelligible: Jesus invokes a mysterious force which is intrinsically *other than* this world. The language of the parables can only approximate to this power – which is why they are metaphors.

Obviously, this is not all that is happening in Mark's Gospel, and I do not intend to discuss here any of the other important theological themes that one finds in that text. But the example of the Markan parables illustrates well the points about language which I am trying to establish: that language cannot encapsulate everything one wants to say about reality, or even one's perceptions of it; even less so when that reality, it is believed, is related to God in God's very being. It also leads directly into this chapter's second important consideration: namely, the possibility of specifically religious language.

2   Is there such a thing as 'religious language'?

Granted, then, that there is no such thing as 'Language', but only different forms of language, which occur in different situations and convey meaning in different ways, the question naturally arises whether or not one of those different ways is inherently religious. Or, if the set of language is made up of hundreds of individual subsets, and one can only think of the set in terms of those subsets, can one say that *religious language* is identifiable as a distinct, independent subset?

To begin to answer this question, one needs to ask an ancillary one: what situation generates religious language? Here a number of possibilities spring to mind. For example, a church (whatever the denomination) hosts certain forms of language which one does not find anywhere else: the Liturgy of the Eucharist, some would say, demonstrates such a peculiarly religious quality. Again, in Roman Catholicism the sacrament of reconciliation is structured around a particular form of language – 'Bless me, Father, for I have sinned' – which makes sense only in the context of Roman Catholic beliefs. And one could say the same of the sermon in an evangelical church. Other examples would be prayer, hymnody, and spiritual and other devotional literature, each of which demonstrates peculiar characteristics which, when brought together, appear to satisfy the criteria of religious language.

The problem, of course, is that the question is unsatisfactorily posed if it is allowed to rest in this fashion. The real question is: is one speaking here of specifically religious language, or of a religious *usage* of certain forms of language and words in given contexts? In terms of what has gone before in this chapter, one would expect agreement with the latter definition. There is, consequently, no such thing as religious language. Rather, what one finds is language, in different settings and contexts, which is used in compliance with the faith of particular groups of people. In this way I preserve the point which I identified earlier: namely, that language is far more of a free-forming, amorphous mass, which settles differently into varying situations, than it is a collection of rigidly defined, independent 'classes', each of which can be identified and successfully characterized in terms of its inherent qualities.

What, then, do I want to assert definitively about religious language? Here an example from philosophy proves illuminating. In the late 1940s, Ludwig Wittgenstein concluded from his analysis of the social use of language that what people do is participate in a number of different language 'games', each of which has different rules and regulations, but all of which engage with language as it is socially constructed. Subsequently, Wittgenstein formulated his specific theory of the language game, which can be illustrated by the following example. Consider a football match. Within the parameters of the football pitch, the players use certain key words and phrases in a particular, universally intelligible manner. Words like 'pass', 'run', 'foul' and so on all have a very specific meaning within the confines of the pitch which they would not necessarily have anywhere else. For example, a pass from one footballer to another is not the same thing as a bus pass or a sexual advance or an abdication of responsibility.

The point here is that language games are small, played and social. By extension, one can say the same thing about other situations. For example, shopping has a certain language game, as have schools, churches, family homes, and so on. Each of these has its own language game, where the word 'game' reveals how one engages with language. One plays at language, actively; and this very playfulness is the quality which makes any action human. It is not a question of being childish, but rather of participating in specific situations and patterns of communication. This is what makes humanity an active and reactive creature, argues Wittgenstein.

With respect to religion and theology, one can make the following observations based upon Wittgenstein's theory. There is no such thing as a subset of language which one can identify as religious language. Instead, there are particular language games within which words and expressions are used religiously. This can mean, as in many of Wittgenstein's examples, that language is understood in specifically functional terms. But Wittgenstein is also aware of what I have referred to as the mysterious side of language: he recognizes the possibility that many of the words and expressions which one finds in a particular language game – as, for example, in the Anglican liturgy of the Eucharist – only point towards meaning and understanding; they don't provide it with copper-bottomed security. This, argues Wittgenstein, is what language is like, an important point with serious consequences for this book and how it understands theology.

What can be said by way of preliminary conclusion, then? First, that there is no such thing as religious language, but that there are many religious language games, within which one can recognize language being used and encountered in a wide variety of recognizable forms. Some of these are easily intelligible, requiring little interpretation. Others are more opaque, requiring considerable co-operation from those who use them to render them comprehensible to an outsider. Each, however, depends upon *context* for its understanding; without a consideration of that context, which means a consideration primarily of social and cultural forms, such language games and the events occurring within them are not genuinely meaningful.

When theology wants to respond to religious language games, what does it have to do? It has to acknowledge that it is not dealing with an object called 'Religious Language', which lies there, inert, waiting for something to happen. Rather, theology must participate in some way in the playfulness of religious language games. It must engage not only with the language of those games, but also with the social and cultural context in which it occurs. And it does this by demonstrating the qualities discussed in chapter 2: by being pluralistic, limited, applied, critical, constructive and imaginative. When coconut theology discusses God's relationship with the world in terms of a coconut's 'face', 'eyes', 'flesh' and 'hair', it is entering into a series of language games indigenous to the Pacific islands, within which the vast majority of those islands' inhabitants 'play' and thereby generate meaning and understanding. That is how coconut theology is a contextual theology.

For theology, handling the building block of language means putting into action the qualities which it must possess in order to be good theology. Indeed, one recognizes theology in action because of the way in which it engages playfully and metaphorically with language games and their varying social and cultural contexts. This makes good theology a matter of *discernment* – of identifying what can and cannot be said to and about a certain situation, on the basis of the Christian faith and addressed to certain people in a certain context. Then discernment leads to action of quality and purpose.

3   What is experience?

Like language, experience has given rise to many attempts to understand it, from philosophers who want to speak about the cognition of sense-data, through behavioural sociologists, to theologians and religious leaders who want to speak of a specific thing known as 'religious experience', by which they mean direct communication from the divine to the human, often in terms of individual relationship. What concerns me here, however, is the same sort of task faced earlier when considering language. It centres on two main questions: (1) is there such a thing as experience? And (2), how do we participate in it? Once these questions have been answered, we can then go on to consider whether or not there is a discrete thing which one can call 'religious experience'.

Initially, I am on safe ground if I argue that probably nobody would want to deny that there are such things as experiences, events in which, somehow and on some level, human beings participate. For example, all human beings experience sense perceptions of some kind: they feel cold, pain, heat, wetness, dryness and so on. Moreover, these are experiences which other animals can have: dogs and cats can experience cold, pain, heat, wetness, dryness and so on. One is speaking, consequently, of sensations which belong to life forms: as long as something is alive, it can have sensory experiences, even if it cannot communicate them.

The next level up from sensory experiences involves reflection upon those experiences, which is where a major distinction arises;

for it is only humans, together with other apes and, arguably, various sea mammals, which seem able to reflect (even in the most rudimentary fashion) upon their experiences. In many respects, this is where one arrives at a more satisfactory and sophisticated understanding of what experience is: it involves sensory perception *and* reflection upon it. This would seem to be common to all people, which makes it an obvious candidate for our prospective definition of experience as something specifically human.

The difficulty, however, is that once again the question of a single definition of something – in this case experience – is mired in the social and cultural issues of what constitutes reflection and interpretation, to the extent that it would seem fair to say that reflection upon experience actually *changes* that experience. Thus, it is impossible to speak of 'Experience' as if it were a giant pie, of which we may all take a piece, thereby having one thing (like 'Language') in common with all other people. On the contrary, there are human experiences, and we all have them, under the constraint of varying cultural conditions. But to go on from that to reason inductively that there is something philosophically ideal which we can call 'Experience' is invalid. Everything we now know of the social and cultural ways in which people live militates against the idea that it is possible to speak of something called 'Experience'. Instead, we are always driven back to the *verbal* form of this idea – experiencing experiences.

This is a useful way of looking at the question of experience, because it throws theology back upon the *practical* considerations of how people live, what it means to speak about our lives in terms of a relationship with God, what criteria we must adopt in order to speak intelligibly and adequately of that relationship, and so on. As with language, therefore, we are justified in speaking of games, in this case experience games, which are themselves intimately linked with language games: we play at experience, following the social and cultural rules or constraints of the context in which we live.

There remains, however, the vexing question of peculiarly *religious experience*: if such a thing can occur, and if it is a direct communication from God to humanity, can we still maintain that such things as society and culture constrain the way in which we reflect upon it, and therefore the nature of the experience itself? If we can, and it is possible for the theologian somehow to engage with this direct religious experience, then this has obvious implications for our understanding not only of theology's questions and experiences, but also of the way in which it works.

4   Is there such a thing as religious experience?

First, I must say as strongly as possible that, given the conviction that God exists, then the possibility of direct communication from God to humanity must be maintained; for not to maintain its possibility (if nothing else) would mean limiting the power, the potential, of God. Some, echoing Barth's theology, might want to argue that God's power *is* limited, and that God has taken this limitation upon Godself in the incarnation of Jesus Christ. But such a strong Christocentric argument has to be qualified by a note of necessary, theological caution; it is impossible ever to be in a position to make such bald assertions. So we are thrown back upon our initial position, that God *may* communicate directly with the individual or community, even though in practice God apparently does not so communicate.

At the same time, I would want to assert very strongly that it is impossible to construct a theology on the basis of a conviction that such a communication has occurred; for, if such communication is genuinely *from God,* how can one express it in words? This is the problem which theology faces when it asks questions about the possibility of religious experience: what is such an experience *like*? How can one *talk* about it? And even if one *can* talk about it, however accurately, how can others understand what it is one is trying to convey, if they have not had the same experience? Speaking of religious experience as a separate 'packet', distinct from all other experience, is impossible, because there is no adequate perspective from which one can say that such and such a thing, feeling or event is a specifically *religious* experience. St Paul confronted this difficulty in his letters to the young church at Corinth, and it is entirely relevant today, which is why the major Christian denominations place so much emphasis upon other forms of authority, such as the Bible and/or tradition. Despite the best efforts of theorists such as Schleiermacher, William

James and Stace, it remains valid that for theology, unlike, arguably, the philosophy of religion, religious experience is not the best authority for theological arguments and doctrinal interpretation.

We are back, therefore, to the problem I identified when asking whether or not it was possible to speak of a peculiarly religious language, and answering 'No': namely, the problem that experience *is* experience, in the same way that language *is* language, and therefore finite and limited. Thus, in order to distinguish one group of experiences from all others, one must be able to identify and communicate what it is that makes that group unique. Since this is obviously impossible for humans when speaking of divine things, the entire question fails, ultimately, to make sense. It is hard for others to make sense of one person's subjective religious experience if they do not share in it. Because of this difficulty, it is problematic for theology, which is public discourse if it is anything, to be established upon the doubtful premiss that religious experience *can* be identified, understood and communicated to others.

Where does this leave theology? Actually in quite a strong position, because the obvious resolution to this problem is to assert that all experiences are *capable* of being religious, because all experiences are part of the world, and therefore part of that which God seeks to address. Thus, the only reliable answer to the question about religious experience is to return to the definition of theology as faith seeking understanding. The faith which seeks understanding wants to say that God addresses the world, *in* the world; hence the conviction that immanence, the concept of God's presence in the world, is central to questions of theological method. This can only mean that anything which is in the world (and so all experiences which people might have) can, potentially, convey something of what it is to be subject to God's address, and thereby be religious. What it does *not* mean, of course, is that there is such a thing as religious experience in and of itself! The distinction is a subtle but vital one, because on it rests the possibility of speaking of God in different ways.

The point here is quite simple but very important. If there were such a thing as specifically religious experience, then theology would be redundant, because where there is sure and certain knowledge and perception, there is no need to seek understanding and interpretation. Ultimately, theology is for people and situations in which religious experience of this purported nature is unknown; where, consequently, mediation is required in the absence of immediate sensation and experience. Theology is a form of such mediation, and as such functions publicly as a means of communicating an understanding of religious belief where normative definitions do not, cannot, apply. This is both theology's greatest strength and its greatest weakness, and it is something which simply has to be learned.

What this means is that theology must relate and respond to both language and experience, and this relating and responding will vary enormously from one situation to another because language and experience are so multi-form, subtle and difficult to pin down via precise, universally valid definitions. Theology is not in the privileged position of being able to deal solely with religious language, or religious experience, as if these smaller and hence more manageable areas existed in such a way as to make the theologian's task simple and straightforward. Theology is *not* simple and straightforward, because *life* is not simple and straightforward. On the contrary, theology reflects the very complexity and diversity of human existence, which becomes most apparent when one wants to speak about language and experience. This is why theology must be pluralistic, limited, applied, critical, constructive and imaginative: because these qualities are all part of being human.

What this does not mean for theology is that anything goes, that just because language and experience are so diverse, taking in all manner of different media and communication, so any type of theology can be constructed, simply because any linguistic expression or experience might conceivably be possible. Although theology cannot, and should not, appeal to specific types of religious language and experience in order to find the necessary authority to speak about God in a certain fashion, this does not mean that theology does not require some authority so to speak. Obviously, authority is necessary in order for a theology to be addressed to its context with any degree of confidence in its acceptance. Precisely what that authority is, however, is a different question.

Where does such authority come from, *if* one cannot speak of religious language and experience? This question will occupy the next three chapters. In Christian theology three main answers are most often given to this question of authority: (1) the Bible is authoritative, because it is the Word of God (as in the theologies of Karl Barth and Rudolf Bultmann, and also in the evangelical wings of most denominations); (2) history and tradition are authoritative (a view one finds in the Roman Catholic and Ortho- dox Churches); and (3) society and culture are authoritative (the perspective which informs many of the contextual theologies which flourish today and which help to shape the popular percep- tion of this discipline). These are functional distinctions, and are not mutually exclusive. But they serve my purpose at this juncture, and I will discuss them more fully in the next three chapters.

- Language and experience are complex things, so that it is intelligent to speak of languages and experiences in the plural. Then one can acknowledge their variety in the different situations in which one prac- tises theology.
- There is no discrete theological language; but there are specific situations in which language with a particular theological character is found. An example would be a church – or a book of theology.
- Similarly, there is no specific religious experience which is the resource solely of theology. Rather, there are experiences which occur in religious situ- ations – for example, the Eucharist.
- However, theology must acknowledge the possibility of a direct experience of God, though it cannot speak of it. Not to do so would mean limiting God.
- Thus, language and experience provide an environ- ment of possibility for theology, but no solutions. Theology works with languages and experiences, but their relationships depend upon other factors.

4

The Bible

- The Bible as criterion and key resource of theological activity
- Definition of the Bible's parameters, acknowledging the distinction between Jewish and Christian texts
- The New Testament's character as testimony
- The question of the Bible's authority as the Word of God, together with understanding of divine inspiration
- The Bible as part of tradition
- Issues in reading the Bible today

There are a number of very simple moves one can make to relate the previous chapter, with its discussion of experience, to this chapter's consideration of the Bible and its place in Christian theology. First, I argued that experiences occur in space and time; that is, they are caused by events and are responses to those events. Second, past events in space and time, as opposed to our present and future experiences, are the stuff of history, because history itself is made up of past experiences, and historical reflection is concerned with understanding past experiences. Third, since Christianity is a historical religion, with a specific origin in space and time, the life and death of Jesus of Nazareth – leaving aside until the next chapter questions about the Incarnation and resurrection – it is reasonable to assume that someone, somewhere, must have reflected upon those origins and spoken/written of their experiences (enter language). Fourth, therefore, one can say that the Bible is, for Christians at least, the prophecy and record of early Christian experience and reflection (language) regarding the life and death of Jesus of Nazareth.

These four simple moves serve to construct a frame of reference which many Christians, and many students of theology, employ to think about the Bible. And these four moves are definite *claims*, which must be considered seriously and tested as the chapter develops. At the same time, however, as being positive claims for one particular understanding – the Christian one – they are negative claims *vis-à-vis* other interpretations, because they contest the claims made by other religions. For example, the major part of the Bible as we have it today is not concerned with Christianity at all. It is about Judaism and its precursor in Israelite faith and society. Simply to imply or claim, then, that the Bible is 'a Christian book', as some do, is to say something detrimental to Judaism, and about one's own self-understanding. Certainly, Christianity claims what it calls the Old Testament as something profoundly meaningful for its own life; but this does not mean that the Old Testament is Christian in origin.

The student must therefore be particularly careful in making statements concerning this building block of the Christian faith and its origins and intentions. This chapter, consequently, is all about raising students' awareness of the sophistication of the Bible, its different books, the questions Christian theology wants to ask of it, and the way it asks those questions. The major subjects to be discussed are: (1) What *is* the Bible, and what is it *not*? (2) What does the Bible set out to achieve? (3) Is it divinely inspired? (4) What is the Bible's relationship with tradition? And (5) How does one read the Bible today? With these questions answered, it should be possible to make some connections between this chapter and the other building blocks of theology.

1   Some parameters

One of the commonest misconceptions about the Bible is that it is one single entity, that there is *the* Bible, which has *one* meaning, and which . therefore speaks of one single thing: namely, the Christian God. In fact, the Bible comprises a surprisingly large variety of different types of text, written under many different sets of circumstances. Discerning its meaning, therefore, is a very difficult task.

This is not necessarily to attack the methodological foundations of an evangelical theology which speaks of *the* meaning of
the Bible. This would only be the case if that theology insisted
that its reading corresponded to the sole, correct understanding
of the text as we have it. If, by contrast, such an evangelical theology acknowledges that its reading is a theological construct, for
the sake and interests of its own context and denomination, then
'the meaning of the Bible' becomes an intelligible proposition.
Again, it is all a question of the *limited* quality of any one theology: a theology is always partial, in both senses of the word.

Before one can begin the task of discerning meaning in the
Bible, therefore, there are a number of steps one must take. First,
it is necessary to make a distinction within the Bible as it stands
today between the Jewish texts and the Christian texts. These are
commonly referred to as the Old and New Testaments in Christian theologies, but for various important and fairly obvious
reasons one should always keep in mind that originally they were
Jewish and Christian texts respectively, thereby preserving something of the dignity of these two very distinct, though intimately
related, religions. The books of the Old Testament span a period
from about 1000 to 300 BCE, 700 years of reflection upon the
Lord's relationship with his chosen people, that people's responsibilities and privileges, and the story of their failures and suc-
cesses in living up to God's loving kindness. It is, then, a
narrative of faith and hope, one which, though adopted by Christianity, remains central to the living faith of Judaism.

Similar things can be said of the New Testament, although it
spans a much shorter period, probably no more than 50 years,
from 50 to 100 CE. The New Testament is the story of the earliest
Christian responses, in community, to the conviction that God
has acted in the world in Jesus Christ, and that thereby its judgement occurred. Because of the compressed nature of this time
period, the New Testament manifests a significant urgency about
the end of the world, something which in Christian theology goes
by the name of **eschatology** – the consideration of the end of
time.

But there are important distinctions to be made within both
the Old and the New Testaments. The former, according to the
traditional Jewish definition, consists of the Pentateuch, the

Prophets, and the Writings. The Pentateuch consists of the first five books of the Old Testament – Genesis, Exodus, Numbers, Leviticus and Deuteronomy. The Prophets are texts concerned with a particular individual's attempt to express what he believes God has told him to say – examples are Amos, Isaiah and Jeremiah. And the Writings are everything else, but perhaps most famously the attempt at a historical narrative of the fate of Israel and Judah, from the entry into the promised land until the destruction of the Temple in 586 BCE, and such texts as the Psalms and Proverbs.

The New Testament is simpler, though arguably as varied, consisting of the four gospels, the Pauline letters to the young churches, some other letters of early Christian leaders, such as Jude, Hebrews and I–III John, and some anomalous texts like the Acts of the Apostles and Revelation. If there appears to be far more inconsistency in the New Testament, this can be attributed to the heightened atmosphere of eschatological hope and conviction in which its texts were written. The New Testament is all about mission, about converting people to faith before the end of the world occurs, and so has a character of great urgency. This still inspires evangelical theologies even today.

It would be wrong, however, to assume that any of the components of either the Old or the New Testament were entirely discrete and self-contained. On the contrary, every such ancient text carries with it questions about its sources, literary construction and possible attribution. For example, the Pentateuch is traditionally attributed to Moses. But considerable Hebrew scholarship acknowledges its origins in a number of different periods and contexts, and speaks of there being distinct layers within the texts themselves. Similarly, the first three gospels of the New Testament – Matthew, Mark and Luke – are regarded by the vast majority of modern scholars as intimately related *at source*: they shared certain documents or orally transmitted stories which preceded the writing of the gospels themselves.

So, 'behind' the Old and New Testaments as one finds them are many different sources; hence one must be careful about speaking of *the* Pentateuch or *the* Gospel of John. Nor is this the end of the story, because apart from all these different writings which were included are others which never found their way into the Bible as we now have it. The Old Testament, for example, does not include the Apocrypha and the Pseudepigrapha, books written outside its allotted time span. Similarly, the New Testament has no place for a text like the Gospel of Thomas, which contains material purportedly relating to Jesus' life and teaching not found in the four authorized gospels. This process of including some things and excluding others, of establishing parameters within which one can speak of authorized texts, was called constructing the canon, and constructing the canons of the Old and New Testaments were two of the most important tasks that ancient believers undertook. All Christians and Jews live with the consequences of their decisions today.

The student of theology proper will be concerned with the reading and interpretation of these texts, with trying to discover their original meaning, perhaps, and what they might mean today. Ancillary to this task is biblical criticism – the discussion and analysis of the historical origins and character of the biblical texts – a discipline which all theologians need to employ to some degree, and with some skill. The issue here is sensitivity to the integrity of the texts themselves: reading them as openly as possible, and recognizing the great variety of styles and questions they generate. Biblical criticism is a very important basis for many theologies – for example, evangelical theologies, which are centred upon a strong doctrine of the Word of God. But it can only be a beginning, not an end in itself. It is a tool to be used to find out more about the origins of the Christian faith as they are recorded in certain documents; but, by its very nature, it is not in the business of theological interpretation. Nor does it respond directly to the principal character of the Bible which is so important for theology: namely, testimony.

In making this distinction, I do not mean that biblical critics cannot be theologians, or that theologians cannot (or should not) write critically about the Bible. Rudolf Bultmann, to name only one example, was a writer pre-eminent in both fields, and in the contemporary world the two are coming ever closer together. Nevertheless, at the risk of sounding old-fashioned, I want to maintain at least a conceptual distinction between biblical criticism and theology proper, if for no other reason than to preserve a place for the attempt at objective study of the New Testament

texts and their reconstructed history. The fact is that many writers
– Ed Sanders is a prime example – explicitly renounce any desire
to write theologically, preferring to concentrate upon objective
analysis. One might mistrust their scientific optimism, but such
analysis is nevertheless an acceptable facet of contemporary scholarship, and as such must be respected. It may not be concerned
with testimony, or with the subtler distinctions of language and
experience. But every student of Christian theology will inevitably
encounter modern biblical criticism in this form.

2   The question of testimony

What, then, is testimony? Testimony is witness to belief; witness
to belief involves reflection upon one's experiences (individual
and social); and reflection and action involve relationships with
others. One can say, therefore, that testimony as witness involves
a communicating reflection and action based on one's experiences, as those experiences invoke one's belief in God. Hence testimony is intimately related to language and experience, the
subjects of chapter 3. In this way, one is justified in speaking of
testimony as *necessary* behaviour by those who claim to have
faith. Theology itself is a form of testimony, as talk about God
and therefore as faith seeking understanding.

As regards the Bible, one can say that both its parts, the Old
and New Testaments, consist primarily of testimony: testimony
to God's actions and what their writers believed to be their
particular relationships with God as well as testimony to how
those relationships have been evidenced in events and experiences. Understood this way, testimony becomes a very useful,
flexible expression in speaking of different forms of religious
communication, particularly the written form which concerns me
in this chapter. It encapsulates everything I said about language
and experience in chapter 3, but now in relation to the texts of
Jewish and Christian origin found in the Bible.

If there is a problem with this idea of testimony, at least in
terms of its application to the Bible and its various components,
it is its very flexibility and seeming universality. It must be maintained that the different texts in the Bible cannot all be absorbed

by one single understanding of testimony, as if 'testimony' itself were a creature which swallowed everything whole. On the contrary, because of the plurality of different texts in the Bible, one must also speak of a plurality of testimonies in those different texts. The books of the Pentateuch testify in a certain way about certain things; each of the gospels testifies about different things in different ways; and so on. This necessary step is designed to protect against the kind of mistake made by early Protestants in the sixteenth and seventeenth centuries, when they talked about *the* testimony of *the* Bible to Christ, thereby reducing the *Old* Testament to the level of a prophecy fulfilled solely and definitively in the *New* Testament. Such a mistake is indicative of a failure to understand the pluralistic nature of all religion and theology.

Thus the Bible comprises different testimonies, and different texts in its two main parts speak of different beliefs. But by what authority do they do this? What authority do biblical texts appeal to in seeking to establish their particular testimony as viable, meaningful and true? Granted that different testimonies *can* be related to each other, if one remembers that such generalizations have limited application, is it possible to speak of *one* specific authority which establishes testimony in itself? This question arises naturally from everything I have said so far in this chapter, and can be considered by asking the question: is the Bible the divinely inspired Word of God?

3   The Word of God?

'Divine inspiration' has a checkered history, particularly in this century. On the one hand, it is taken to be *meaningful* in some sense – it conveys something of the special nature of a classic religious text, and so is permissible. On the other hand, it is rejected as the last refuge of religious fundamentalism, a phenomenon one recognizes, evocatively, in the 'Bible Belt' of the United States. This tension between what one wants to say about the divinely inspired status of a diverse religious text like the Bible and how that understanding may then be used by fundamentalists goes to the very heart of the question of authority. In particular, the important issue here is how 'inspiration' (however one defines it) is believed to be communicated from God to the individual or community.

How is 'inspiration' defined? Inspiration means direct communication from God to the individual, who then (in the case of a literary text) writes down what has been communicated. Depending upon the degree of clarity attributed to the initial communication, that process of writing down can be taken to be effectively *dictation* – 'God said it to me this way, I wrote it down' – or *suggestion* – 'God moved me, and this is what it felt like'. At all points, however, whatever degree of urgency one wants to give to the communication itself, the real point here is that a direct, immediate message from the divine is received and *recognized* as such. One is not dealing with a mediated sense of religious meaning, as anyone might receive when experiencing a religious **symbol**, such as a church or a liturgy. Rather, one is dealing here with the close corollary of 'religious experience', knowledge of the intelligible (because communicating) presence of God.

It is this claim to knowledge which gives the notion of divine inspiration its real power and which ultimately makes it a corrupting force in *theology*: it is knowledge, or better still *information*, which makes a particular form of religious discourse, such as the Bible, potentially *the* dominant authority in a historical context. An example of this is found in first-century Judaism, the world of the New Testament, where apocalyptic – the seeing of heavenly secrets – flourished in many different forms, decisively influencing the prevailing socio-political aspirations of the Jewish people under Roman law, and effectively leading to the rebellion of 66–73 CE and the destruction of Jerusalem. Apocalyptic claimed to provide precise information about what was going on in heaven, and particularly about God's plan for the world: so it promised power to those who could access it.

In many respects, contemporary fundamentalism's appeal to biblical inspiration is very similar to first-century apocalyptic, with the proviso that for the latter there was always the possibility of new revelation, whereas for the former the process of revelation has been closed (by God's will) by the formation of the canon. Hence it is impossible for people nowadays to claim divine inspiration in the way it is predicated of the writers of the Bible, because the latter have special status, and the only people who come close to that are those entrusted, by dint of their special calling from God, to articulate what the Bible means today. A self-perpetuating circle is thus established: contemporary authority is established by biblical authority, which in turn reveals the root foundation of contemporary authority: namely, the Holy Spirit. A good example of this was Martin Luther who, when challenged by papal authority to abandon his theology of justification by faith alone, famously refused, stating: 'Here I stand; I can do no other' – *because* he believed that the point he was making was the selfsame point that Paul was making in his Letter to the Romans, and because that theology was vouchsafed by the Holy Spirit.

Theologically this is a very difficult area, which the student of theology is well-advised to treat cautiously, because there is no way of judging with any degree of certainty whether or not somebody has had a genuine religious experience, still less of deciding whether the biblical writers were so divinely inspired that they took down the Word of God *verbatim*. Instead, theology should focus on the question of authority itself, asking: how can one speak of the authority of the Bible in such a way that it remains a fluid, open point for discussion in contemporary theology, without becoming closed off in the limited language of *verbatim* inspiration? Some might argue that this question is self-serving, designed solely to preserve the otherwise redundant role of theologians themselves – but there is an important point here: to what extent can theology meaningfully address the question of the continuing authority of the Bible? How can the Bible be, today, the Word of God, if one is unsure of how to speak of divine inspiration?

One viable answer to these hard questions is to speak of the Bible as the Word of God in terms of believers' *responsibility* towards God's professed intent within their faith and practice. Theologians must consider the ways in which teaching the Bible points people towards living better lives, orientated towards the Kingdom of God and the return of Jesus Christ (for Christianity). The Word of God, then, is one of responsibility: it defines a particular form of Christian conduct, one founded in human experience, and one witnessed to by the biblical writers. For Christian theology there is nothing else: all genuine questions of authority, of knowledge and of information wilt in the face of the question of responsibility. This was the point made by Karl Barth against liberal Protestantism in 1919 and following, and subsequently by both modern Roman Catholic and Protestant theologians.

Is the Bible the Word of God? Yes – but that conviction is meaningful only to the extent that this mystery of faith is made pertinent to the lives of individuals and communities. Words, including the Word, must be spoken; speech must be heard; hearing must be interpreted; interpretation must be acted upon. For theology, if not for all forms of practice, therefore, the most pertinent task is to continue the process of speaking, hearing and interpreting which has itself been going on for over 1,900 years, and which continues today wherever Christian communities meet to speak of their faith and its consequences for their lives: namely, the Christian tradition.

4   The Bible and tradition

Like inspiration, 'tradition' is regarded by many as a loaded word. Indeed, one can almost speak of inspiration and tradition as mutually exclusive antitheses, the former favoured by broadly evangelical groups, the latter by the Roman Catholic and Orthodox Churches. In theology, however, talk of inspiration always limits; theology falls silent when confronted by the absolute claims to authority of those who covet divine inspiration. Tradition, by contrast, should always liberate theology to raise afresh the experiences and reflections of those who have gone before in the faith. Tradition is their story, and as with all good stories, it is the suitable and necessarily humble discussion to which all churches and communities can appeal. No one in Christianity, therefore, is ever alone. Even if God is not felt to be present, there is always the communion of the brethren who have fallen asleep.

At least ... this is how tradition should be interpreted, devotionally, and how it should then inform theology. That it does not, however, is another sign of that human weakness which always appeals to certainty ahead of responsibility. On this reading, the unsatisfactory definition of 'tradition' regards it as a monument to the true meaning of both *the* faith and *the* Bible. Tradition is, therefore, the *deposit* of truth about these things which has been systematically mined from the original sources. On this reading too, theology is assumed within the general archaeological task: the theologian 'digs up' truth, using his or her critical tools to find out what things really mean. On the whole, communities which adopt this definition of tradition and theology have little real time for the latter, because for them it is far more important to preserve the former.

From what I have said previously, the student will appreciate that I want to criticize this understanding of tradition. Instead, I want to speak of tradition as something alive and vibrant, dynamic and changing, within which all Christian individuals and communities live, and to which they must all contribute as they grow and develop and hope for the realization of God's rule in the world. Tradition, consequently, is never closed; it is the open vessel into which all Christian individuals and communities pour their experiences and reflections. Theology does not simply live *from* tradition, therefore. It also lives *towards* tradition. And in so far as tradition always successfully manifests its dynamic quality as the home of any faith which seeks understanding, so theology can speak with justification of tradition's own authority as the principal *raison d'être* for speaking of God.

On the basis of this understanding, one can make an important point about the relationship between the Bible and tradition. The Bible is to tradition as text is to interpretation. But since the Bible itself is a (written) interpretation of human experiences of, and reflections upon, a relationship with God, then one can say, decisively, that the Bible is also part of the tradition. Thus, the Old Testament is itself traditional in so far as it is part of the continuing narrative of God's relationship in time with God's chosen people, the Jews; the writing down of stories about this relationship is a traditional act, because it testifies to the continuity of faith and understanding within that religion. Similarly, the New Testament is traditional: it testifies to God's action in Jesus Christ, and at the same time adds to that action by itself being part of the gift of the Holy Spirit, poured out upon the Church at Pentecost.

On this understanding, the Bible, like tradition, is both text and interpretation: the two combine as they witness to, and constitute,

Christian testimony to God's continuing relationship with humanity. Thus, notions like 'text' and 'interpretation' (and indeed 'Bible' and 'tradition'), which readers must be aware of because of their important role in providing structure to theology, give way to the overriding social and personal concerns of continuing in the faith, of being responsible for practice and actions, and of seeking not knowledge, but understanding. This is all that Christian theology can fairly and reasonably be asked to do: to seek understanding. There are no definitive answers in theology, therefore; there are only better ways of asking the same questions which Christians have been asking for nearly 2,000 years.

When I am asked, then, to define theology, I can point both to the qualities discussed in Part I and to the responsibilities towards language and experience and the Bible so far considered in Part II. But at the same time I must answer that theology is not something which stands *beyond* any of these issues. Rather, theology exists within things: within language and experience, within the Bible, within history and tradition, within society and culture. What I am engaged in, consequently, in writing an *introduction* to theology, is trying to show people some of the major ways in which theology is involved in so many of the normal aspects of everyday life. Naturally, theology is also outside certain things; it is outside God, for example. But socially one can speak meaningfully only of theology's context, of what it is within, so by far the most important thing is theology's place and location. Today, theologians everywhere are struggling to justify their place in society, which is why it is so important to understand how one's definition of theology relates to one's definitions of language and experience.

The task of the student of theology is to understand how theology finds its way inside the central building blocks discussed in this section, and how it relates to things outside the faith. As an illustration of this process, and as a way of ending the present chapter, I turn to the task of reading the Bible today.

5   Reading the Bible today

By 'reading' here, I do not mean biblical criticism, something I discussed briefly earlier in this chapter. Biblical criticism is its own discipline, and the way in which a biblical critic attempts to read a text is very different from the way in which a theologian reads one. Reading here means interpreting, and interpreting means adopting a position with respect to the building blocks of the Christian faith. This, ultimately, is the main task of theology, and Part III will have much more to say about the structure and dynamics of how this task can and should be undertaken, and how theology goes about the business of interpreting its raw material – doctrine. At this stage, however, it is possible to make some pertinent comments about interpreting the Bible, which will be relevant to the more general discussion to follow.

First, as I indicated earlier, it is not possible when reading and interpreting the Bible in all its different forms to speak of 'the meaning' of the text; there is no single thing called 'the meaning of the Bible' which one can simply pick out of the text as it stands. Instead, such reading and interpreting requires a subtle and sophisticated procedure. It must be responsive to the particular circumstances of the text, and to the specific needs of the individual or group reading and interpreting. Otherwise, one is left with simple repetition, which, as with many simple things, is not possible.

Second, and consequently, reading and interpreting the Bible generates many different understandings of its various meanings, because different meanings will be the result of the different situations in which people read and interpret, and in particular *what* in the Bible they read. This is where tradition comes in, because on a simple analogy tradition was, and is, the sum of all the different readings and interpretations, and therefore of all the different meanings, of the Bible which have been regulated and evaluated by the authorities of the Church, a process which in the early Christian period – until 451 CE – was carried out via the Church's councils and **creeds**. Thus, reading and interpreting the Bible always was and is, a vital part of defining what the Christian faith was, and is. Otherwise, one could not continue to maintain Christianity's identity as a historical religion with specific origins.

Third, and finally, this entire process of reading, interpreting and discerning meaning in the Bible, which was so important in the early Christian period and which was integral to the Church's actions of self-definition in canon, creed and council, continues today, as Christians in different parts of the world read and reflect upon what they find in Christianity's historical origins, what it means in terms of religious belief, and how it relates to the world in which they live. This is what reading implies – testing the meaning one finds in the world in which one lives. And because theology is an applied science, it is also a reading science in this sense of the word. Theology reads the Bible and tradition, in search of meaning about God. But it also reads the world, in search of meaning about what it is to be human.

Many of the implications of this understanding of reading and interpretation will be considered in chapter 10, when I look at modern and contemporary developments in theology. Before that, however, I want to say something about the historical foundations of tradition, about the 1,900 years of experience and reflection which it contains, in greater detail than has been possible in this chapter. Chapter 4 flows into chapter 5, then. But in the next chapter I want to ask, in much greater detail: what does the tradition *contain,* and how is this related to *history?* This will help to contextualize many of the things I have been saying about the Bible, as well as introduce some of the social and cultural categories which will become central in chapter 6.

- The Bible is a shared book, and therefore theology must be sensitive to its importance for Judaism.
- Similarly, the Bible comprises many individual texts, reflecting many different situations and communities. This makes its theological interpretation today a matter of great sensitivity.
- This is illustrated by the Bible's characterization as testimony, and by its traditional status – biblical texts confess a faith which was part of the tradition before the Bible was created.
- The Bible's status as Word of God is a question of authority and hence power. 'Divine inspiration' cannot be proved, but solely confessed. For theology this is a question of interpretation, not demonstration.

5
History and Tradition

- The antecedents of contemporary theologies in past theologies, with particular respect to history and tradition
- Definitions of history and tradition, with specific reference to Christian interpretations and usage
- Tension between evidentiary and interpretative understandings of history and tradition; development and role of the latter in the history of Christianity (patristic, medieval, modern)
- Discussion of problems involved in understanding history and tradition, and their role in theological activity

Each of the two previous chapters examined an area of theology which most students will recognize, because of its obvious significance for religions in general (language and experience) and Christianity in particular (the Bible). Thus, the first two building blocks considered in this part of the book are clearly relevant for anyone trying to understand how theology works: believers speak about the Bible, language and experience, because that is where they think God addresses humanity. The simplicity of this model is not imaginary: certain Christian denominations in the world, such as the Religious Right in North America, adopt this way of doing theology. And in general, as we have seen, certain evangelical theologies are highly effective communications of a fundamentally biblical faith, with important and profound practical implications for the communities and churches which practise it.

The present chapter, however, introduces two new elements, history and tradition, which are not so obviously relevant to theology, and which require quite a lot of preliminary definition before one can get to grips with some of the more sophisticated questions and difficulties associated with them. Moreover, as many students will recognize, 'tradition' is a loaded term. It has an ancient significance for the Roman Catholic and Orthodox Churches, which constitutes a real distinction from those churches which advocate solely the Bible or solely religious experience as the basis of authority (though without denying the importance of these last two). Consequently the student will encounter some new developments in turning to consider history and tradition: not only questions of intra-faith dialogue between denominations with very different theologies (which has been touched upon in previous chapters), but also, with respect to history, questions relating the subject matter of Christianity to secular events.

In what follows the reader will find some initial definitions, followed by two longer sections which develop a more sophisticated understanding of why theology should be concerned with history and tradition (respectively), how theology profits from the association, and its meaning for the interpretation of faith in the world at large. Then, in a concluding section, some of theology's difficulties with regard to history and tradition are anticipated, together with suggestions as to how the reader might consider their contemporary role in theology. After all this, the chapter's significance for an understanding of society and culture will provide a link with the next chapter, and the culmination of Part II.

1 Initial definitions

1.1 History

What is 'history'? This question, so often implied, is rarely asked out loud. Instead, people throughout modernity, and throughout contemporary society, seem entirely happy that they know what history is. It is either (1) a realm of past events or facts which is growing ever larger as time goes by and the present itself becomes past; or (2) a type of research which is concerned with past events or facts, and which is pursued by people who are interested in the past in and for itself. History is thus something which deals with 'hard' information (data), which in turn is established by observation, reading documents, digging up building sites and so on, and which then provides a picture of some aspect of the past which is historically accurate because it fits the facts.

This definition of history, which reduces it to a hyper-accurate 'instant snapshot' of the past, was established during the Enlightenment in the eighteenth century, when philosophers advocated the power of reason to identify scientifically the past events and causes which form the social basis of the world in which we now live. On this reading, history is concerned with such things as the French Revolution or Julius Caesar's conquest of Gaul or Copernicus's realization that the earth revolves around the sun. In theology this approach is well illustrated by the quest for the historical Jesus, in which nineteenth-century critics (predominantly German) attempted to 'discover' the 'real' Jesus hidden by 1,800 years of dogma and tradition. Needless to say, as Albert Schweitzer so brilliantly demonstrated, all they succeeded in creating were their own dogmatic images of Jesus, every bit as theological as anything preceding their 'quest'. Realizing the status of such images is an important step towards greater understanding for the student of theology.

There is, of course, a place for such an attempt to recover the past in objective terms, no matter how doomed to failure it must always be ultimately; for the attempt says something important about the scientific manner in which people understand history. More recently, however, people have come to see that history is not simply concerned with reporting brute facts. On the contrary, it is concerned also with the ways in which people understand and interpret not only facts, but also the world in which they live. Thus, history is about the informed stories which people tell about their origins, beliefs, social customs, practices and so on. Interestingly, the German word for story, *Geschichte*, is the same word that German uses for history when understood in this sense. The history of facts and data is designated by the word *Historie*, and a modern German theologian such as Rudolf Bultmann in this century made much of this distinction, arguing that theology should be concerned with *Geschichte*, not *Historie*.

Broadly, this is the perspective I want to advocate here. History *is* about what happened in the past. But one cannot know and understand what happened in the past without considering questions of interpretation, story-telling and how people understand their own lives and world. Much of this will sound familiar to readers who have worked their way through the previous chapters, particularly where I have spoken of the need to be flexible in approaching the tasks and responsibilities of theology. History benefits immeasurably from a flexible approach; that is how it becomes important for theology.

1.2   Tradition

Tradition is different from history, yet similar, because tradition is also concerned with what is past and with its meaningful interpretation with reference to the way in which people live their lives in the present. 'Tradition' is a word used theologically to denote the body of doctrines, creeds, catechisms, articles and definitions which has accumulated over nearly 2,000 years of orthodox (non-heretical) Christianity, and which today exerts a powerful influence upon what one says and does not say about God. In many cases, this powerful influence manifests itself as specific doctrine, as a hard-and-fast rule that such and such a thing is right and all others wrong. An example of this in Roman Catholicism is the doctrine of papal infallibility which, though comparatively recent, has rapidly become a test of faith in some situations. And again, evangelical theologies would place great emphasis upon the biblical provenance of a stated argument – for example, the doctrine of the Church.

Technically – and fruitfully for theology – tradition should be something which grows and develops as the Christian faith and its understanding grow and develop in the world; tradition in this sense cannot be fixed or limited, because there will always be new things to add to it. An example of this is the way in which liberation theology in Latin America has added to the tradition the idea of Christianity's preferential option for the poor, attempting thereby to give it normative value, at least in that particular context. This emphasis is something which, liberation theologians argue, one finds in the earliest New Testament writings. Similarly, feminist and womanist theologies around the world are developing and adding to the Christian tradition, often by remedying distortions of interpretation introduced by previous (male) interpreters. This is both necessary and fruitful for contemporary theology.

In practice, however, tradition is (wrongly) understood by many theologians and Church figures to be a closed book: something to which nothing can be added, and from which nothing can be taken away. On this understanding, tradition becomes something sacred and therefore to be protected, rather than something vital and living, to be interpreted and developed. And when this occurs, the result is that someone must assume the responsibility of providing such protection. This is what one sees so often, and so sadly, in the history of the Christian tradition: people appeal to it as the sole, definitive authority for their arguments and actions, forgetting that tradition itself is only meaningful to the extent that people live their faith and bear witness to tradition as the story of others who have tried to do the same thing.

What one must always do, therefore, is bear in mind that tradition is about the way in which Christians over the years have lived out their faith. Certainly, it is about what great Christians of the past have considered to be right and wrong, and one must respect that aspect of its character. But it is also about the way in which Christians live their faith today and will live it tomorrow. Tradition is alive; and alive like theology, it bears witness to attempts to understand faith. Good theology always returns to this issue sooner or later.

2   History and theology

Returning to history, let us pick up again the question of the historical Jesus and consider what it tells us about the relationship between history and theology. On the one hand, there is the question of 'what Jesus was really like', which depends upon certain facts. This question is important for evangelical theologies. On the other hand, there is the question of what one might say about Jesus today, theologically, which may be very different from 'what he was really like'. An example of these two emphases would be the historical analysis of Mark's Gospel, which indicates that Jesus was angry with Peter at Caesarea Philippi, so much so that he called Peter 'Satan' (Mark 8: 33), versus the fact that many theologies down the centuries have spoken of Jesus' overwhelming love and kindness, as if he could never be angry with anyone. There is, then, a tension here; how should it be resolved?

The short answer is that it cannot be resolved: Jesus' anger towards Peter comes down to us through the testimony of an evangelist, Mark, who was operating with his own and his community's set of religious beliefs, and who consequently constructed his own theological image of Jesus. Jesus' anger and Jesus' kindness are equally theological motifs, so the tension of which I speak is a creative one, rather than something which can be reduced to empirically verifiable data. The characterizations of Jesus one finds in the New Testament are not history in the sense of hard-and-fast data. They are stories, and as such have story-*tellers*, and audiences, who inevitably hear things differently.

Obviously, it would be wrong to suggest that history is not concerned with questions of true and false, right and wrong. History has an important role to play in determining what is right or wrong with one's theological stories and images, so that if one propagates an erroneous impression of, for example, Jesus' character, one which is demonstrably wrong according to historical evidence and research, then one does so knowing that there will be something amiss with one's results. For example, Adolf Hitler's conviction that Jesus was really an Egyptian can be demonstrated to be wrong simply by reading the relevant texts carefully and in a disciplined manner. Similarly, history can help theology by producing a certain body of reliable information, which theologians can then take away and use to inform their stories and images of God – for example, about first-century Palestinian Judaism as Jesus' world. In this respect, the history of theology since around 1780 (when historical research in theology really started to grow) has been extraordinarily rich in its development and use of research and data. We know and understand far more today about the origins of Christianity in first-century

Palestine than we did even 200 years ago. The discovery of the Dead Sea Scrolls, for example, has played a significant role in this process.

The same can be said of history's value for theology's appreciation of its past applications – for example, during the patristic, medieval and modern eras of Christianity. Thus, we know far more today than we used to about the characters, movements, ideas, controversies and beliefs of Christians who are now dead, knowledge which allows us to make much more informed judgements about the theological ideas we might want to invoke today which have earlier echoes in attempts to understand faith. As the student will recognize, this means that history is important for an appreciation of tradition, because the more one knows about the deliberations of one's predecessors in the tradition, the more one can understand and interpret the ideas and arguments and, in some cases, regulations which one finds therein.

There are, however, certain drawbacks to this otherwise rosy picture of the relationship between history and theology. For better or worse, theology cannot simply be historical and report such facts as when things occurred, what their apparent causes were, who was responsible, etc. Theology is more than simple reportage. It is about being creative and imaginative, constructive and critical, limited and applied, qualities which would be largely irrelevant if theology were simply a matter of 'getting the facts straight'. Such a reduction, moreover, would deal a fatal blow to all those theologians who want to think historically about questions of origin and cause, and who believe that history has many lessons to teach contemporary theology concerning the meaningful interpretation of the Christian faith. 'There is nothing new under the sun,' runs the adage. But if it is *literally* true, what can the future of theology be?

This acute problem is more significant today than ever before, and its different aspects can be identified by considering, once again, the case of liberation theology, which in part is rooted in a historical understanding of the New Testament's stories about Jesus of Nazareth. Importantly for liberation theology, it is possible, on the basis of historical-critical research, to identify the key ingredients of Jesus' message about God's will and its expression in the gospel as the Kingdom of God. For liberation theology those key ingredients are all intimately related to questions of social, political and economic import, so that it is possible to argue, on the basis of history, that the Kingdom of God is about effective change in the material circumstances of the poor and oppressed. In this way liberation theology gives authority to history to establish theology's agenda, so that, if it is not established by historical research, then it finds no place in the work of liberation theologians.

Obviously, if it were possible to verify such information with certainty, then most theologians would accept it. The real problem, however, is that, as with any historical analysis, one often finds solely what one is looking for. Liberation theologians, because of their own convictions and responses to the societies and cultures in which they live, look in the New Testament for 'evidence' which fits their arguments, and overlook material which does not fit. This phenomenon can be found in the work of such historically aware theologians as Leonardo Boff, Jon Sobrino and Edward Schillebeeckx – all significant Roman Catholic figures – with obvious implications for the way in which one evaluates their work. It does not invalidate their arguments, but selective quotation is a very particular type of **hermeneutics**, and one which is easily challenged by people who attach importance to other biblical passages.

The real difficulty in the relationship between history and theology, consequently, is not so much whether evidence can be verified or falsified (though this is important). It is, rather, that any form of historical analysis is inherently selective: it discovers what was already present in its own methods of investigation. It is like wearing a particular set of spectacles to look at a particular question: what one sees will always be framed by what one is looking through. The historical Jesus one 'sees' in the New Testament is always conditioned by the Christ of faith one 'sees' in one's belief and community. So historical research is forever destined to view events through the spectacles of historical research itself, rather than with the perfect vision which it so often supposes it possesses.

There is no way around this difficulty. Rather, history, and indeed theology, must simply accept the situation. It is possible to be reasonably certain about many facts concerning both the origins of Christianity and its development during the first few centuries of the common era; one need not be entirely relativistic. But this does not mean that it is possible to construct theology solely upon such factual foundations. As with many things in theology, methodological problems require compromise; and compromise is a process of argument and counter-argument which one recognizes in the history of Christianity.

3   The development of tradition

Compromise: the ability to mediate between two apparently antithetical positions, maintaining the best qualities of each without siding with one or the other. This quality is supposed to be evident in democracy and its twin, politics, where it goes by the name 'consensus. It is a quality which one finds also in the development of many movements throughout history, such as the establishment of the Athenian democracy, the Roman Republic, the modern British monarchy and the American Constitution. It is not, however, a quality often associated with the development of the Christian tradition.

What do I mean by this? Simply that compromise is not something which marks out the debates which have raged throughout the 2,000 years of Christian theology, which, on the contrary, have been distinguished by the antitheses of **orthodoxy** and **heresy**. When one defines ideas in terms of orthodoxy and heresy, one does not encourage compromise, one encourages division; and it is division which has marked, sometimes in physical terms, the development of tradition. The most obvious example is the separation of the Eastern from the Western Churches for the last 1,000 years, a separation which has its roots in tradition and its interpretation. But similar tensions exist today between the liberal and evangelical wings of Roman Catholic and Protestant denominations in North America and Europe.

Some other examples will demonstrate this point more fully. The definition of the New Testament canon in the third century – which texts were to be included and which excluded – aroused fierce debate, with different schools of thought almost coming to blows over certain texts. But the solution to this was to establish

definite parameters which silenced opposition. Similarly, the
Council of Chalcedon in 451, which established the orthodox
doctrine of the two natures of Jesus Christ, was a triumph for the
Alexandrian over the Antiochene school: by validating one
particular understanding of Christ's being, Chalcedon established
the tradition decisively, with lasting effects on Christology.
Finally, the split between Martin Luther and Roman Catholicism
in 1521, which precipitated the ensuing division between Protestantism and Roman Catholicism throughout the world, ultimately came down to a matter of translation – whether or not
Luther's addition of the Latin word *sola* ('alone') to Paul's doctrine of justification by faith was legitimate or not. Each of these
examples says something important about the manner in which
the Christian tradition has developed.

Development itself, therefore, is a process. And as with many
processes, it is dialectical (see **dialectic** in Glossary): it moves
from a conflict between hypothesis and antithesis, towards synthesis and thereby resolution. In this respect, the development of
the tradition is a story of movement towards synthesis, towards
compromise – but a sense of compromise which is marked by
argument in its resolution. What has characterized this process of
conflict has been what one might call the quest for criteria of
judgement, ways of making those difficult decisions which deter-
mine the development of tradition. Again, this returns the discussion to questions of authority, because criteria of judgement
require clear authority if they are to be accepted. The reason why
Luther refused to recant before Rome in 1521, after all, was
because he refused to acknowledge the authority of the Pope
against what he regarded as the greater authority of Scripture.
'Here I stand; I can do no other,' stated Luther solemnly; but he
believed he stood upon a sound judgement of the meaning of the
New Testament. The same can be said of many contemporary
theologians: for example, Pat Buchanan and Jerry Falwell of the
Religious Right in the United States.

What does this say about the development of tradition? That
we are mistaken if we regard that development in purely linear
terms, if we think of it as a simple sequence of cause and effect,
in which hypothesis is overtaken by antithesis, leading painlessly
towards synthesis. On the contrary, this is the romanticized

vision which was rejected in defining history; for on this point, history and tradition are intimately related. Thus, just as it was impossible to speak of history simply in terms of seamless movement, so tradition, because it is historical, cannot be regarded in this way. Tradition is historical, and being historical, it is victim to those dynamic forces of collision and conflict which have shaped the proclamation of the Christian faith throughout its existence.

Tradition, therefore, is the collection of witnesses to the historical events which have befallen Christianity over nearly 2,000 years; but these are very special historical witnesses, and consensus was never achieved easily (as remains the case today). Instead of being made up of factual accounts of events and episodes which have changed and developed social and ecclesial institutions, like the lists of data one finds in, for example, the archives of local government, tradition is constituted in, by and for arguments and practices, because it is arguments and practices which govern the way in which one seeks to interpret faith. In this respect, the Christian tradition constitutes less of a history book, and more of a story, in which the principal themes and characters are defined not by their appearances, but rather by their ability to convey something of the meaning of Christian faith.

Nor, it follows, can tradition be regarded as a document, preserved by an unknown authority but within which one can discover everything one needs to know about Christianity – a theological Constitution, perhaps. On the contrary, the tradition is the opposite of a theological compendium. Indeed, it does not *exist* at all, in any material sense. Rather, it, the tradition is more a 'self-regulating creature' than a 'thing'. In the light of human reflection at crucial moments, it establishes, alters, removes or restores ideas which are all intended as ways of speaking meaningfully about God. If it is beginning to sound as though tradition has a life of its own, that is because it has, which is where difficulties arise.

4   Some anticipated difficulties

It is possible, then, to become too romantic about tradition. After all, its relationship with history means that it is eminently controllable, doesn't it? Actually, no; if anything, we are controlled by tradition. History, we may like to think, is safe because it has clear and distinct boundaries. And so, by and large, it has – if we accept the standard definition of history as something which is past – which means that it is, by and large, reliable and discrete. But tradition does not possess such parameters; tradition is not past. Rather, tradition *is*.

What this means is that theologians and readers have to make a choice between allowing this liberal definition of tradition its autonomy, with the result that it becomes almost impossible to speak of anything other than traditional theology, and resorting to the classical distinction between orthodoxy and heresy which would, at a single blow, separate tradition into two distinct parts. The advantage of the latter is that it is conservative in the best sense; it conserves what is most important in traditional Christian theology. Its principal disadvantage, however, is that the state of contemporary theology militates so strongly against its reintroduction that battle-lines are now being drawn up and defended by progressives who perceive in it nothing less than the re-emergence of the old orthodox hierarchies. Far from being a dead letter, consequently, history and tradition constitute one of the live debates of contemporary theology. This can be illustrated, for example, by the way in which contemporary feminist and womanist theologies are reinterpreting the New Testament, specifically with a view to hearing the 'hidden' voices of women's testimonies.

Thus students will have to make some considerable methodological decisions as they come to grips with the business of studying theology. It is not a matter of 'What do we agree with?', but rather 'What criteria of judgement do we adopt in making decisions about how we speak of God?' The real issues here reduce to questions of authority, because it is the search for authority, and its responsible management, which defines any intellectual discipline, be it theology or philosophy or any other science. Authority and responsibility: these are the twin pillars of decision making with regard to theological method.

There is more to the story than even this, however. The four chapters of this section, concerned with the four building blocks of theology, have looked at four separate areas of responsibility for theology. But these four areas are not simply building blocks in a passive sense. They are also potential bases upon which one might construct theological models. And, as with most building blocks, one does not need to adopt all of them simultaneously. One can choose between them, just as different denominations emphasize different authorities and responsibilities. All this opens up for discussion the distinct possibility that the only real solution to the problematic question of tradition is to ignore it entirely.

And indeed, some adopt this attitude: for example, the Religious Right in North America, identified at the beginning of this chapter as an evangelical movement with a strong emphasis upon biblical authority and personal religious experience, has relatively little interest in tradition in and for itself. On the contrary, the few times when it has concerned itself with 'traditional values' have been when making explicit appeals to the ideology of 'home and hearth', as at the Republican Party Convention in Houston, Texas, in August 1992. Similarly, the broad reach of Protestantism, including both the Lutheran and the Reformed varieties, places far greater emphasis upon the Word (particularly the New Testament) than it does upon tradition, which in any case has suffered a major breach, in Protestant eyes, by the events of the Reformation. Finally, various contemporary theologies, such as feminist, black and political theologies, which set out to overturn present injustices, are actively opposed to tradition, which they regard as the natural parent of prejudice. Many of the theological books which you are likely to pick up will demonstrate one or other of these attitudes, and there is no guarantee that you will ever come across what might be called a historical or traditional book of theology today.

Does this mean that history and tradition are irrevocably relativized for contemporary theology? By no means; it simply means that one can no longer grant to them the absolute authority which they enjoyed in earlier periods. Instead, their authority must be argued for, the strongest argument for the authority of history and tradition being the responsibility of the contemporary reader and theologian to those who have gone before them. Christianity is, after all, a historical religion, and one, moreover, which demands and expects intelligent responses from its adherents. And if theology is faith seeking understanding, this confers upon it a special status. If for no other reason than an awareness of other Christians, then, theology is duty-bound to consider history and tradition.

If these themes receive stronger advocacy here than elsewhere in contemporary theology, it is because I recognize the lack of such historical and traditional reflection in contemporary discussion, to its loss. Nevertheless, it must be acknowledged that the overriding concern of contemporary theology is not with the Bible, or with history and tradition, or even with language and experience. Rather, it is with society and culture. In the final chapter of Part II, therefore, I will examine society and culture as the seemingly most relevant contemporary building blocks in theology.

Before that, however, it will be useful not only to recap the arguments of this chapter, but to look at how they relate to the argument of the book as a whole, because then certain key ideas can be summarized. First, it is clear that history and tradition are difficult to define, and that even when satisfactory definitions are constructed, it remains uncertain whether contemporary theology wants to be concerned with these matters. Certainly, the student of theology must be aware of history and tradition, and their place in theological discussion. But whether or not this is ever translated into historical or traditional theology is another question.

Second, it is apparent that this is also the case with the Bible, which was the focus of the previous chapter. Again, although students must be aware of the role of biblical interpretation in theology, they may well never come across it in the books they read. There is, consequently, something of a crisis in contemporary theology, in which classical forms of the discipline are being slowly squeezed out by the more topical issues deriving from culture and society.

Third, this development raises important questions for the methodology of theology. Can one now speak of *the* task of theology, as chapter 8 does? Can one now speak of *the* shape of theology, as chapter 7 does? Certainly, these things will be argued for in Part III; but the student must keep a very open mind as to whether or not they are *possible*.

Fourth and finally, therefore, the last part of this book (IV) consists of two chapters, reflecting the split nature of contemporary theology: on the one hand, a strong concern with the classical themes and subjects of Christian theology; on the other hand, a commitment to the radical development of the subject under contemporary constraints, which may challenge its very status *as* theology. For now, these things remain open to question and debate; but by the end of this book they will require an answer.

Before that is possible, however, Part II must complete its discussion of the building blocks of Christian theology, which means turning to society and culture. Once again, questions of definition will be at the forefront of my argument, as I establish a clear foundation for the way in which theology relates to these things.

- For theology, history is not about facts; it is about stories and how they are interpreted. Tradition, made up of Christian stories, is thus a process of historical self-interpretation by Christians. As such, it takes many forms.
- On this understanding, tradition is a process rather than an object; it is something of which contemporary theology forms a part, as earlier theologies also formed a part.
- Contemporary theologies are themselves therefore historical and traditional, as they engage in self-interpretative processes within specific contexts and situations. Christian history (patristic, medieval, modern) demonstrates this process at work.
- One major question arises, however: by what authority and criteria can any one process of self-interpretation be justified? Each contextual theology must answer this question for itself.

6

Society and Culture

- Definitions of society and culture as immediate environment of theologies
- Examination of the social character of theology's audience, particularly its significance for practical questions
- Marginalization of culture in modern theology and its restoration as a principal theme in contemporary theology
- Consideration of society and culture as necessary for the broadening of theology's agenda; their role in shaping theology's self-interpretative activity

The previous three chapters have addressed the obvious resources of theology. One expects theology to 'use' language and experience, the Bible, and history and tradition; these are the 'stuff' through which the relationship between God and humanity is generally understood. Moreover – and whatever I have said about the need to interpret these things in relation to all the others – there is still the understandable determination to examine the Bible, for example, on its own, to regard it as uniquely *the* resource of theology, giving it the recognizable splendour of isolation. In this way one can see why biblical theologies occur, and why such things as historical, traditional and experiential theologies, too. There is nothing inherently wrong with any of these approaches, and communities engaged in each of them can be found within most denominations. But it is impossible to argue that any one theology is right *per se*.

With society and culture, by contrast, other questions come into play. We are not dealing here with discrete entities, open to exclusive employment. On the contrary, society and culture are global matters, relevant to everyone: we all live socially and we all participate in cultural events – witness buying and reading this book. In many respects, society and culture are so huge, and so amorphous, and they contain so many tiny, individual societies and cultures (rather like Wittgenstein's language games), that it is safer and more meaningful to speak instead of situations and experiences as being social and cultural. This is the sense in which I use these words here: as qualifying adjectives, rather than monolithic entities.

This is not anything new, of course. Every church in every denomination makes decisions about its relationship to social and cultural matters, just as it makes decisions about political and economic matters. When theology comes to consider its relationship with society and culture, therefore, its responsibility is towards everyone and everything. It is not possible to close off certain areas of society and culture, saying explicitly or implicitly that these are theology's sole concerns. Theology cannot possess society and culture, as it might claim to possess the Bible or its own history and tradition. Rather, it is possessed by society and culture; theology is social and cultural. This should also be said of language and experience, of course, and theology can never really think that it simply 'takes hold' of such things, 'from the outside', as it were. But it is particularly true of society and culture, because when one speaks of the relationship between theology and, for example, society, one is moving into the important area of theology's practical implications. Or, to put it in question form: what effect does theology have?

The fuller implications of this question will unfold in the two chapters of Part III, but here some preliminary aspects are considered. Specifically, this chapter examines the social nature of all theology, its comparative neglect of culture in the past, and the way in which society and culture help shape theology as a means of human reflection. Then we will be ready to move on to the task of theology, to be considered explicitly in Part III.

1   All theology is social

Many people will remember a statement by the then Prime Minister of the United Kingdom, Margaret Thatcher, during the 1980s: 'There is no such thing as "Society" ' – a comment which helped to reinforce her own particular understanding of religion as exclusively private, and therefore as having nothing really to do with what groups of people might contemplate or achieve – a view largely shared by Ronald Reagan. On the Reagan–Thatcher model, one might argue that 'No theology is social'. But the heading of this section is '*All* theology is social'. Why?

The simple reason, as Aristotle pointed out, is that human beings are social beings; we instinctively gravitate towards groups and communities. People come together in identifiable crowds and communities, be they clubs, towns and cities, or tribes and nations; consequently, specific forces come into play which affect these people *as* crowds and communities. (If one doubts this, consider the things which affect people when they are in a crowd at, say, a football match, things which would not affect them if they were watching it on television at home: the noise, the weather, three dimensions not two, etc.) To argue, therefore, that all theology is social is to argue that theology is inextricably involved with these specific forces, because they are relevant to the way in which people live. And it is 'the way in which people live' which theology needs to address, as it witnesses to, and seeks to understand, the Christian faith. If theology does not relate to the way in which people live their lives, then it is not, on its own terms, theology, but something else.

This begs an obvious question, because the way in which people live is not a simple matter to identify, evaluate, measure and act upon, as we have seen in our reflections upon language and experience. On the contrary, it requires detailed examination, analysis and interpretation; it requires a skilled consideration, such as sociologists, economists and political theorists undertake as part of their everyday working lives. Theology, consequently, must be one such science among others if it is to take seriously the complex nature of society and the various forces which help to shape people's lives, fears and aspirations.

Theology must learn from, and be guided by, society and by other ways of understanding society; it is a discourse *of* the world and *about* the world. A good example of this is the way Paul went about the business of establishing new churches in the Gentile world: as his letters demonstrate, the issues confronting Christians in Corinth were different from those in Rome, or Galatia, or Thessalonia. But it is of great importance for Paul *that* such social questions are addressed.

This is also what one finds if one considers the world of contemporary theology. For example, in the liberation theologies of South and Central America, which argue that God's Kingdom as proclaimed by Jesus Christ is intended to overthrow the oppression of the poor in the world, one often finds detailed analysis of the social, economic and political factors affecting people, with theology interpreting these factors in part in light of what influential secular writers have to say. The most oft-cited example here is Karl Marx, and it is true that broadly Marxist analysis has proved enormously influential with certain liberation theologians. But to claim, as their critics have, that such theologians are in thrall to Marxism, is untrue. What liberation theologians are doing is allowing their work to be informed by secular theory (for example, Marxism, though this is not the only theory influencing them), so that their theologies become more effective in addressing the truth of God's Word to the world in which they live. This is not something partisan or biased. Rather, it is an acknowledgement of theology's responsibility to respond to the social nature of human existence in a particular situation.

Something similar occurred in South Africa, where various theologians, such as the Dominican friar Albert Nolan, attempted to address the oppression of blacks and coloureds by whites under the apartheid regime (and are still working on its effects, after the 1994 democratic elections). Here it is not so much a question of economic analysis, such as one finds in South and Central America, as of political analysis, although politics, like economics, is always part of social thought, and so the comments made above apply also to the political theologies of South and southern Africa. Similar stories could be told about political theologies in North America, South-east Asia and Europe – in fact all over the globe. Wherever a theologian reflects upon the relation-

ship between God and the world, there social reflection also
enters.

As the reader will hopefully appreciate, these emphases relate
theology to the social nature of its responsibilities, with respect to
language and experience, the Bible, and history and tradition. If
theology is social in itself, then it follows that it will understand,
for example, the Bible socially. Theology will want to regard its
major resources and responsibilities from the perspective of
society; in the same way it will want to view society itself from
the perspective of society. This is how theology can be genuinely
practical, and thereby genuinely able to address the specific concerns of people's everyday lives. Without this emphasis, theology
is always in danger of slipping into irrelevance.

All this implies that theology, which is broadly theoretical and
therefore concerned with looking at problems, must always be
seeking a way of moving towards what is practical. It must
always look for a way to test its ideas and thoughts, to *do* theology, in order to find out whether or not what it is saying has any
meaning for the way in which people actually live. This is an area
of theological reflection which greatly concerns many students,
understandably, and which has therefore taken on almost normative status in the eyes of most people over the last thirty years.
Its contemporary significance indicates an impatience with theory
per se – of the kind often found in earlier, more classically ori-
ented, times (up until the late 1960s in theology) – and an urgent
need for practical theology *per accidens*. My argument, of course,
is that all genuine theory is of practical import, and therefore that
all genuine theology is practical theology; but this does not militate against the call for active theologies which we hear all around
us today. On the contrary, what it means in effect is that a
Western theology, for example, should be explicitly addressing
such issues as abortion, IVF treatment, human sexuality, and the
rights of gays and lesbians, and so on, as its day-to-day business.

The ethical implications of this position are hard to ignore, and
by and large I want to endorse this stance as the necessary implication of arguing that all theology is social. At the same time, it is
important that theology's responsibility towards society and the
practical questions that raises be balanced by recourse to theology's other resources, from which it learns of the Word of God.

Theology is pulled in two directions, and although there is a way of steering between the two poles, and looking in both directions at once, this tension must be recognized. It will undoubtedly affect the way in which one encounters the subject in one's reading and study.

2   The marginalization of culture

This tension between theory and practice has dominated the history of modern theology since the late eighteenth century, and shows no signs of abating. Indeed, in Roman Catholicism it is a major issue when it comes to understanding the place of liberation theology within the Church. There has always been one area, however, where this tension has been mediated and a way found which speaks to both concerns, and that is culture. Hence it is a consideration of culture which can provide a way forward at this stage. Remember, though, that by 'culture' I mean not so-called high culture, but what is of a cultural *nature*, and that cultural experiences and entities are small and specific, rather than large and general. Particular examples will make this point clearer.

In the twentieth century, the intimate relationship between theology and culture has been advocated by two notable theologians: the liberal Protestant Adolf von Harnack (1851–1930), and the Roman Catholic Hans Urs von Balthasar (1905–89). Harnack adopted an optimistic view of this relationship, regarding the essence of the gospel, and therefore God's will, as being realized in the high social, educational, ethical and cultural achievements of Prussia and, after 1870, Germany. Such things as art, music, literature and classical education, in so far as they mirror the qualities Harnack recognizes in the humanity of Jesus, are able to realize God's will in the world. Thus culture – for example, in the form of Bach's *St Matthew Passion*, or Grünewald's Isenheim altar-piece, or Goethe's *Faust* – has a unique ability to communicate the glory of God. But, more importantly for Harnack, it means that the age, and particularly the people, whose achievements these are, have a special relationship with God. One can see how such an attitude would create difficulties for a *German* theologian in the first third of the twentieth century, where the identification of God's will with the fate of Germany had such tragic results for so many people during the Hitler years, 1933–45.

Hans Urs von Balthasar also spoke of 'discerning the form' of God's presence in culture, particularly the high art and literature of Western Europe. Von Balthasar has been spoken of as 'the most cultured man in Europe', and if 'culture' here is restricted to the very narrow confines of what is sometimes dubbed 'high culture', this may even have been true. Unlike Harnack, however, von Balthasar did not speak of the peculiar status of the German people or culture. Rather, his major concern was the mediation of grace through aesthetic achievement and appreciation. For von Balthasar it was axiomatic that cultural achievement is good; it was also axiomatic that God is revealed, however indirectly, through what is good. Thus, God can be revealed through culture. Alongside revealed (biblical) and natural theology, therefore, von Balthasar gradually elevated aesthetic theology to a significant position in mid- to late-twentieth-century Roman Catholic theology. Today we can see the effects of his influence, with theologies now taking seriously the role which cinema and drama, music and literature, have to play as media of religious and theological meaning. Rock stars like Madonna, U2 and REM, as well as being enormously influential, also have an iconic status which is open to theological interpretation – as have films like Steven Spielberg's *Schindler's List* and, less seriously, Walt Disney's *The Lion King*. Assessing their relevance is one more job for the student of theology.

Apart from these two figures (and to some extent Paul Tillich), however, twentieth-century theology has been reluctant to speak of God's indirect revelation through culture. In fact, one is justified in speaking of the marginalization of culture as theologians have attempted to discuss theology in terms, overwhelmingly, of knowledge and understanding – that is, as entailing epistemological and hermeneutic issues. It is almost as if twentieth-century theology had subconsciously decided, after about 1920, to abandon all but the most conventional means of speaking about God's activity in the world and society (von Balthasar, significantly, was not part of the theological establishment). Undoubtedly, in this respect the influence of Karl Barth was far more pervasive, and Barth's metaphysics of the Word as sole medium of God's revelation has dominated Protestant theology to the present day, with a very specific impact upon the latter's character and ambitions.

Was this marginalization in any way justified? Even on a cursory reading, the answer must be 'No'. Granted the implication of late-nineteenth- and early-twentieth-century culture in the rise of fascism in Europe, this does not implicate culture *per se*. On the contrary, it implicates the abuse of culture, of which its marginalization is another form. What is required, therefore, is a theological reappropriation of culture – an acknowledgement that God's will can indeed be mediated and revealed through broadly aesthetic means.

Why? Because culture is an important aspect of any society. In a literal sense, culture 'grows on' society, thereby manifesting some of society's most important aspects. Cultural theory can thus illuminate some of the most important social themes and forces upon which theology should reflect: aspirations, fears, imagination, reverence, disgust, conformity, anarchy. Whenever these social forces are expressed culturally, they become political; they become important for the way in which society is structured and ordered. For theology to ignore culture, consequently – 'popular' as well as 'high' culture, the point holds for both – is for it to ignore some of the clearest outward signs of the forces which are shaping society and the people who live in it. Even off the top of their heads, most people can think of examples to illustrate this point: the growth of punk rock music in 1977, the escalating budget deficit in the United States in the 1980s, the Irangate scandal, the Waco siege in 1993, the growing acceptance of graffiti as an acknowledged art-form, the developing interest in opera in the 1990s as people become steadily enculturated by television, the challenge to traditional sports by new leisure opportunities. Each of these illustrates the general point I am making here.

All these examples, and other serious ones such as the women's rights movement, demonstrate that culture in a wider sense is more than von Balthasar realized, and more, therefore, than simply the high points of art, music and literature. It is essentially anything which demonstrably expresses the feelings of people in society, and is therefore very specific. Culture, then, is not an abstract concept, which is the impression one can receive from reading some philosophers and theologians. Rather, it is an astonishing mixture of diverse media and appearances, all of which say something about the social life enjoyed (or suffered – again, consider graffiti) by people at large. If theology ignores these media and appearances, even if it pays great attention to economics and politics, it will not fully understand the forces at work in society; it will not be able, then, to address liberative words and actions towards people yearning for salvation. This has been the case with too many churches and theologies in the modern era for it to go unnoticed in the 1990s.

3 Responsibility to context

Responsibility to context, therefore, involves the theologian in listening and watching. Good priests and ministers know this instinctively: witness the heightened social awareness one finds, for example, amongst both Roman Catholic and Protestant priests and ministers in Northern Ireland, as in inner-city ghettos in the United States. It is something that theologians, however, must cultivate as energetically as possible.

How do theologians watch and listen? The simplest answer to this question is that they must participate in their society and culture, because only through participation will they acquire the necessary data for the theological responses which people need and find useful. When theologians fail to participate in and be aware of the activities, emotions and expressions of the world around them, they start producing desiccated theology: rather like someone rearranging dried flowers, their 'art' or 'science' is reduced to the level of a formality, something concerned with structure, but not with the dynamic which gives life to any model. Much of the tension in modern theology has centred on this problem of structure and dynamic.

Even the theologian who demonstrates this necessary awareness and participation, however, may paint too rosy a picture of their world, dramatizing its qualities for the sake of addressing its

potential and aspirations. Theology can easily become too optimistic, equating utopian dreams of society and culture with the
Christian message of the Kingdom of God. When this happens,
questions of truth are too easily identified with questions of
method, so that an understanding of how to proceed theologically becomes too easily a definition of God's being and will.
Arguably, one can recognize this tendency in certain forms of
contemporary theology, such as liberation, feminist and green
theologies, where the one overriding issue at stake becomes normative for all theological arguments.

The antidote to this tendency (which may be intelligible but is
ultimately destructive) is to emphasize the prophetic role of theology – its task, as with the prophets of the Old Testament, to
address not only the positive aspects of the world in which the
theologian lives, but also the negative ones. Today, theologians
generally do not like to do this, too commonly regarding it as
destructive rather than constructive. The point, however, is that
being constructive also means being critical, which in turn means
addressing the failures of society and culture to live up to the
ethical and eschatological goals of the Christian faith. Certainly,
such critical address is not the only means of returning the problems of society and culture to the agenda. But for Christian theologians it is fundamental.

Traditionally – for example, in the New Testament – this criticism of the world is made in terms of sin – people's turning away
from God and the revelation of God's will. It is a question of
drawing attention to humanity's failures, in the conviction that
such failure is contrary to God's will, and therefore blocks or
hinders Christ's work of revelation, rather than simply attending
to the positive things that people do socially and culturally, and
the possibilities of realizing God's will on earth, and moving
towards the Kingdom of God.

A theologian like Karl Barth, writing in the middle of this
century and therefore against the background of two world wars,
placed tremendous emphasis upon the Christian understanding of
sin, so much so that the doctrine of the Fall – humanity's complete alienation from God – played a crucial role in his theology;
the existence of sin ensured the necessity of grace, by which alone
humanity could be redeemed in Jesus Christ. In contemporary

theology, however – for example, the liberation theology of the Jesuit priest Jon Sobrino – sin is located more specifically. For Sobrino, the sin of society and culture is to be found in the exploitation of the poor and oppressed in Latin America by the multinational corporations and their partners in government. He speaks, therefore, of 'structural sin', which can be redeemed only by 'structural grace', where 'structural' refers to the way in which sin and grace are built into the fabric of society. In this way Sobrino relates the traditional Christian themes of nature, sin and grace to the particularities of his own social and cultural context. Such theologians as James Cone and Cornel West have put forward similar arguments concerning black theology, with signal importance for the contemporary study of the discipline.

This approach has many advantages, given the circumstances which these theologians are trying to address. The problem, however, is, that by weighting the question of sin so much in terms of the admitted evils of racism in the United States, for example, Cone and West have little to say about the personal sin of the people they want to champion. Thus – and this is typical of liberation theologies in general – they say relatively little about the sins of the oppressed: it is as if the oppressed are not them-selves sinful, but solely sinned against. This may well be the line that black theology or any liberation theology wants to take in its interpretation of the gospel. But the question is whether it will suffice as a general model of the way in which theology should function. It is an open question, but relevant.

All this raises the shadow of theology's inadequacy to work on all the levels to which it is called. Theology simply cannot carry the weight of responsibility to society and culture which it must attempt: it is pulled in two antithetical directions, with the result that it tends to split. To keep this from happening means recog-nizing the inadequacies of theology, and operating with a model of its structure and dynamic which calls explicit attention to its frailty. In connection, I now want to turn my attention to the implicit, and therefore omnipresent, partiality of theology; for this partiality is at one and the same time both theology's strength and its weakness.

4   The 'spectacles' of theology

First we must ask what 'partiality' means in this context. Obviously, relating this question back to what I said in chapter 2, we can say that calling a theology partial means admitting that it is limited and applied; but it also means something more. It means admitting that theology is not only limited and applied, but also *biased*: biased both towards God's Word of revelation and God's sacramental presence and also towards the specific context in which a theologian writes and works. Writing for a specific situation also means, at this level, writing *against* others. As a theologian, one's writings cannot be universally applicable to every situation. That would be to negate the diversity of God's creation, a diversity which manifests itself in the very specific social and cultural circumstances in which we all live.

This is easy to say, of course, but difficult to take on board in practice, because in so far as theology seeks to address the universal God, does it not also seek to say something of universal significance about the world? This is the line that the Congregation of the Doctrine of the Faith of the Roman Catholic Church adopted when it suppressed Leonardo Boff's writings in 1985 because of his alleged distortion of the Roman Catholic doctrine of the Church and its teachings, through the appropriation of Marxist theory. Boff's case – that he was writing for the people to whom he ministered – was acknowledged by Cardinal Ratzinger. But Ratzinger also pointed out the implications of Boff's position, as critical of the Vatican, and therefore, in the eyes of Rome, contrary to the teaching of the Christian faith. Boff, consequently, was silenced, not because he opted for the poor, but because he was perceived to be implicitly opting against the Vatican.

Leaving aside the question of whether or not one thinks that Rome was right in Boff's case, this episode relates to the question at hand in a very precise way. Granted the responsibility which any theologian has *vis-à-vis* such things as the biblical witnesses, tradition, language and experience, and society and culture, where can the theologian find genuine authority? To a degree there is universal authority, which resides in the witness of faith and the power of the Holy Spirit (as Christianity believes). But in earthly terms, where else does authority genuinely reside? Cardinal Ratzinger's argument, as we have seen, is that it resides in the Church, meaning Rome. But to what extent can this be true for all theologians, operating as they do in many diverse situations, with the widest range of specific pressures and tensions, duties and obligations?

Here I would argue that the overriding authority of the theologian, granted the integrity of their respect for the biblical witnesses and tradition and their appeal to the power of the Holy Spirit, must be located in their own particular social and cultural context. If they are validated by their own community, to whom they address their theology, then such theologians have an authority to continue their work, at least until their fault is demonstrated in dialogue with other Christian communities. Though there is, consequently, an important question regarding the authority of the Church in general, which has implications for such matters as **ecumenism** and interfaith dialogue, nevertheless a theologian must obtain authority from the community which they seek to serve, and which endorses their work by testing its worth. Without this local, inherent authority, derived from being part of a specific society and culture, the imposition of a foreign authority, which transcends everyday reality, cannot work. This is especially true of the extremely diverse societies that make up the West, where an appreciation of their composite character is vital.

In this sense one can speak of any theology as being conducted through the particular 'spectacles' of its world and community. It sees nothing without the aid of these spectacles, which shape and focus its perception of whatever must concern it. Consequently, there is no sense in speaking of the perfect vision of theology, as if theology could see, under ideal circumstances, everything it desired to see, thereby being enabled to identify and address the fundamental nature of the relationship between God and humanity. On the contrary, theology divorced from its context in society and culture is rather like a mole – weak-sighted almost to the extent of being blind. Seeing through spectacles makes theology workable; and after all, there is no point in a theology which does not work.

All this means that being a theologian, or studying theology, can be an infuriating business. It can be very restricting, because it is not simply a matter of telling people what one thinks the Christian faith is. On the contrary, it is about addressing a whole host of different questions and situations, many of which may not seem particularly relevant, but all of which are fundamental to the continuing, historical life of Christianity and its many diverse communities. The greatest of theology's responsibilities, in many ways, is to society and culture, because, as I have argued, without these two, theology is simply so much conceptual acrobatics. It is therefore vital that contextual theologies continue the work they have begun.

My conclusions at the end of this chapter, therefore, are also my conclusions to this section as a whole. They return us to the question of how one defines 'resource', which I answered by locating it in the arena of theology's various responsibilities. This has helped to reveal something of the important duty of theology towards its subject matter. At the same time, however, this tactic has dodged an important question, namely: to what extent is a resource or building block simply something with which to build? What about the apologetic or defensive role of theology? These two questions rest upon the conviction that theology cannot simply be a positive force, moving out into society and culture, interpreting the Bible and tradition, being aware of language and experience, and so on. Rather, it must also say, and construct, something which will last. It must make something of the resources at its command.

This question opens the Pandora's box of the task of theology to interpret and the raw material of contemporary theology as doctrine and its understanding, which will constitute the subject matter of the next two chapters. Here, however, I can give a preliminary answer, at the same time opening up some of the questions of Part III which the student will have to consider.

First, the task of theology is indeed constructive: it creates models which further our understanding of the central ideas of the Christian faith and communicate them to the members of a specific community. Thus theology does build things; it does have a product, one which can be tested and evaluated, and one which will, ultimately, be superseded by the 'latest model'. Such is the nature of the beast, and by recognizing this fact at the outset, the student of theology has a much better chance of understanding the machinery of the various models which will be encountered.

Second, these models must conform to certain important standards, because there are 'colours', 'styles' and 'features' which are so important to any understanding of the Christian faith that they cannot be ignored or omitted from any model, whatever the context or denomination. A very simple example is Jesus Christ himself: a theology which failed to mention Jesus would be a very odd interpretation of the Christian faith. There arises, consequently, the question of scale in theology: models have to be big enough, and uniform enough, to address a wide variety of circumstances and communities, even if they say many of the same things in many of the same ways. In this respect, the resources and responsibilities of theology discussed in Part II help to ensure that the production line of theological models has certain recognizable standards of continuity.

Third, this continuity must itself be extended to the matter of the product of theological models: namely, doctrine and its inter-pretation. Thus, doctrine as product must have certain recogniz-able marks which say 'This is Christian' to the listener or reader, so that he or she can be confident that such and such a doctrine is genuine – for example, that Jesus Christ was crucified. This means that the process of testing doctrine and interpretation bears marked similarities to the quality control machinery which many companies establish, which is necessary to ensure that good-quality models and products are put on the market and that the paying public is not short-changed (which some would argue has been the case in theology for far too long). Without pushing this metaphor too far, it is possible to speak of the corporate nature of Christianity, and theology's role as what is essentially, at least here on earth, a manufacturing company.

Each of these issues will return in Part III, where chapter 7 examines the nature of doctrine as the raw material with which theology operates, and chapter 8 considers the task of theology to create interpretative models. As with each chapter in this book, I will draw on earlier examples and arguments to develop the new themes to which I now want to turn.

- All theology is primarily social: though it acknowledges the individual's questions, its principal audiences exist in groups (communities).
- Culture is central to theological activity, because theology finds expression through a wide variety of cultural forms: poetry, literature, dance, music, etc.
- Paying attention to society and culture is a key aspect of theology's showing responsibility to its context: it constitutes the 'spectacles' through which the theologian views the world.
- Theology is thus a hermeneutic activity: its parameters cannot be preset, but are discovered via the process of interpreting socially and culturally.
- Thus theology is one discourse amongst others; and its practice can be understood by analogy with other forms of discourse.

PART III

Developing Necessary Skills

Part II was designed to introduce the student to four central areas wherein are found Christian theology's resources and responsibilities. Underlying my treatment of these themes and questions lies an enormous amount of material, some of which students will come to know well, some of which they will never discover. This is simply a fact of studying any discipline at higher-education level: it involves a certain amount of processing information which characterizes the subject under discussion. It is an irrelevance to discuss whether or not this is a good thing: it simply is the case.

Throughout this book, however, I have been at pains to point out to the student that theology is not simply, or even primarily, concerned with processing data; though there are several good textbooks which supply a great deal of information, this is not where the heart of the discipline lies. As with any applied science, rather, theology involves a great deal of practical work. It requires the student to become involved not solely with the nuts and bolts, but also with how those nuts and bolts fit together. I discussed the prerequisites for this practical approach to theology in chapters 1 and 2. Now in chapters 7 and 8 I want to examine the mechanics of doing theology.

I name Part III 'Developing Necessary Skills', thereby emphasizing my argument that theology is straightforwardly a discipline which can be taught to anyone. It is by no means esoteric, the preserve solely of the few, but is open to all who can adapt to certain reflective requirements. In chapters 7 and 8 I name those requirements as doctrine and interpretation. I want to outline here why they are important, and why they are central to the topic of Part III.

If theology is a learned skill, it is a skill which Christians have been practising for nearly 2,000 years. Because of this, it is imperative that students appreciate that they are conducting experiments that others before them have conducted for centuries, and that the results of those experiments have been tested and retested and, to the satisfaction of many, have stood the test of time. They have become doctrines, and the Bible and tradition are replete with the evidence of the results as people have mastered the skills required to be theologians. Paul, Augustine, Aquinas, Luther, Schleiermacher, Barth: in a very important sense, students today are learning to practise the same skills as these theologians in earlier generations.

Simultaneously, however, those skills are intensely contemporary things: they require students literally to look around and relate the central themes of Christianity to the situations in which they live. This is crucial to the future viability of theology as a discipline – that people acquire and practise its focal skill by thinking about the way they live. That skill I name 'interpretation', and in chapter 8 I show how it supports many of the discourses we find in the world.

Part III, therefore, carries this introduction to theology forward, away from matters of resource, towards questions of application. The most important emphasis here is on the student's own ability to think through the issues and questions which arise. That is the skill that must be acquired.

7

Doctrine: The Shape of Christian Theology

- Definition of doctrine and of the Church as
  authority for its creation and interpretation;
  illustration of this process in the history of tradition
- Socio-linguistic rather than propositional or
  experiential character of doctrine; coincidence of
  this character with the nature of practising theology
- Questions of openness and closure of theology as
  doctrinal interpretation
- The theologian and the shape of theology today, as
  defined by Christian doctrine

Openness and flexibility characterize contemporary Christian
theology, where a strong consciousness of the pluralistic nature
of the modern world, combined with a deepening awareness of
the contextual character of theological argument itself, enables
theologians to interpret the Christian faith and message for their
particular situation much more sensitively than previously. This
is not to argue that contemporary theologians are paragons of
virtue, or that earlier generations were mired in darkness and
ignorance. But in general my point stands: as theologians and
students of theology, we are now in a different age, one in which
questions of methodology – of *how* theology works as a social
science – are acquiring increasing significance. Theologians like
David Tracy, in his book *Plurality and Ambiguity*, and Avery
Dulles, in his *The Craft of Theology*, have addressed just such
issues.

This argument points towards chapter 7's specific agenda,
which is to define Christian doctrine as the shape of theology.

Just as the qualities discussed in chapters 1–2 shaped the way in which we considered the building blocks of chapters 3–6, so that material is in turn shaped into the specific doctrines of Christianity. Or better, *was* shaped; for the original work of fashioning the doctrinal position of Christianity was undertaken by the early Church. That is where this chapter will begin.

1   The Church as authority

By 'the early Church' I mean the Church during the period beginning with Paul's letters to young churches, the acts of the apostles (however one defines them), and the writing of the first gospel, around 50–70 CE, to the Council of Chalcedon in 451, the greatest ecumenical council of the early Church, where the fundamental doctrine of the two natures of Jesus Christ was pronounced orthodox. This is a very straightforward definition, found in nearly all of the many textbooks on this period of Christianity's history. This period is sometimes known as the 'patristic period', because it was characterized by the activities and texts of the early Church 'Fathers' – although today the expression is criticized by feminist theologians.

Mention of the Council of Chalcedon here is important and useful, because this period to 451 was one of considerable strife and contention, of debate, argument and indeed violence as differing groups and parties within Christianity struggled to dominate their opponents in matters of understanding, interpretation, definition and practice. Each of these conflicts was about power and authority: whose way of talking about a particular question – be it the humanity of Jesus, the nature of the Church, or the relationship of Father, Son and Holy Spirit – was the right one. And just as power and authority are intensely practical matters, even when centred upon apparently theoretical and abstract concerns like the divine 'substance' (a suitably vague term for something nobody can possibly identify), so the early Church became, almost by definition, the forum wherein conflict was resolved, the defining locus of theological power and authority, with consensus emerging only after years of struggle, violence and dissent – with implications still felt even today.

A simple example will illustrate this point. From the time of Paul and Mark onwards, theologians argued about the nature of Jesus' relationship with God: whether he was inspired, possessed, an angel, the Son of God but less than the Father, or the Son of God and the same as the Father, and so on. Individuals like Tertullian and Origen in the second and third centuries put down markers for subsequent generations, most of which were later condemned as heretical; but it was not until the first quarter of the fourth century that the debate reached a climax. Then a theologian called Arius argued vehemently that the Son was a created being subordinate to the Father, exploiting the vagueness of the prevailing definition of the Son's relationship with the Father to make his point. Arius thereby threw the early Church into crisis.

Going more deeply into the debate to develop my argument, Arius exploited the Greek word *homoiousios*, meaning 'of like substance', used of the relationship between the Father and the Son, to argue that these two were not of the *same* substance; for if they are of *like* substance, then obviously they are not of the *same* substance. This was the point at which the mainstream Church attacked Arius when it decided to respond. (I will not make a value-judgement about substance language, which looks inadequate to contemporary eyes. Suffice it to say that it was thought appropriate and meaningful in the patristic era.)

What strategy did the Church adopt when it decided to attack Arius and his ideas? Remember that the central point was the status of the Son: was he of the same substance as the Father, or not? In deciding that he was, the Church selected a very simple action by which to announce its collective decision, ensure the loyalty of the majority of Christian churches, and condemn Arius and his followers: it promulgated a creed in which the statement 'of one substance' – *homoousios*, not *homoiousios* – was predicated of the relationship between the Father and the Son, demanding that all orthodox Christians adopt and swear by it. This was the Nicene Creed, formulated at the Council of Nicaea in 325. Failure to accept this creed resulted in excommunication – the fate of Arius.

The period from Nicaea to Chalcedon, 325 to 451, was characterized by the gradual adoption of the *homoousios* clause in other important areas of Christian doctrine or teaching, such as those relating to the Holy Spirit and the Trinity, and theologians like Athanasius and the Cappadocian Fathers – Basil the Great, Gregory of Nyssa, and Gregory of Nazianzus – employed it quite rigorously to authorize and ultimately enforce their arguments. Indeed, one can argue, without too much fear of contradiction, that the identification and endorsement of the *homoousios* clause was a defining moment in the development of Christianity towards its most stable form. With one word, literally, it erased several of the crises threatening to engulf the early Church in division and anarchy.

Expressed in black and white on the page of a textbook over 1,600 years later, these debates seem curiously arid and vague, so it is hard to imagine how and why they were so important to so many ordinary people in the fourth and fifth centuries. But the key to appreciating their significance is to think about what the terms 'the Church' and 'council' meant. It is easy to write that 'the Church selected a very simple action by which to announce its collective decision', as I did a few moments ago. But what does it mean? It means that a certain group of theologians and church leaders, representing a diversity of churches and communities, came together to attack, by means of a council and a creed, another group of theologians and church leaders, representing their own followers and communities. These two groups met at Nicaea to debate the differences between 'of like substance' and 'of one substance', which is the distinction most textbooks focus upon. But they also met to try and find a consensus about what they thought was *true*, and what authority that truth might have. What then happened is that one group of theologians had the emperor Constantine on their side; and they won, because Constantine favoured 'homoousios'. An important aspect of the story of Nicaea, leaving aside the theological implications of the choice of technical terminology, is that of power and authority. Or, to put it in the terms of Part II, social and cultural issues shaped decisively the development of tradition, thereby changing the nature of subsequent Christian language and experience.

Today, theologians speak confidently of 'the doctrine of the *homoousios*', by which they mean the teaching of Nicaea as it has come down to us to the present day. What they seldom acknowledge, however, are the practical effects that this teaching had upon people immediately after 325, the way in which their lives were changed by their acceptance or rejection of this one word. What one finds today, though, is the same process of appeal to, and exercise of, power and authority in differing Christian churches. One example is the recent decision by various churches of the Anglican Communion to ordain women as priests, which has affected both relations within Anglicanism itself and its relations with Roman Catholicism. Or one might cite the debate within Roman Catholicism about contraception, where the explicit power and authority of Rome to control the lives of its members is wielded – and challenged – daily. Both are examples of the way in which *doctrines* – the teaching of the Church on a given issue or question – become the focus of debate and tension regarding the power and authority of the Church in question, a situation which continues, as witnessed by contemporary debates about theological understandings of human sexuality, for example.

Why do doctrines have this effect? Because they function as *parameters*; they *limit* the way in which one can, officially and in an orthodox manner, speak of something. The doctrine of the *homoousios* is one such example, because it limits – even if quite creatively – what one can say about the relationship between the Father and the Son while remaining within orthodox Christianity. Similarly, the doctrine of Christ's two natures – that he is equally and indivisibly God and man – limits what one can say about the person of the Saviour. What *else* one might say about Jesus Christ, *in addition to* his two natures and one substance with the Father, is open to interpretation, something we will see in greater detail in the next chapter. But *that* one endorses the two doctrines here identified – this is fundamental to orthodox Christian theology. It states that Jesus Christ is truly human and truly divine – and as such the identity of God and the world.

It would be wrong to suggest that this is the whole story with regard to questions of power and authority, and many theologians today would argue that notions like 'orthodoxy' and 'the Church' are obsolete. But the student has to start somewhere, and the mainstream position is usually the best. Thus, doctrines are limiting concepts, designed to communicate the parameters of what has generally been identified as acceptable teaching about a specific issue or question. But what else are doctrines?

2 The nature of doctrine

In 1984 the American theologian George Lindbeck published a book entitled *The Nature of Doctrine*, which stimulated considerable debate for several years. In it Lindbeck argued that the two most frequent ways of defining a 'doctrine' – propositionally, as something akin to a conceptual law, and experientially, as a teaching derived from life – were unsatisfactory. People do not govern their lives according to concepts, argued Lindbeck, and personal experiences, though certainly valid and meaningful for those having them, were, well, *subjective*: how could one person's experience be normative for a much larger group, or indeed for something called 'orthodox Christianity'? – hence, Lindbeck provisionally concluded, the poor state of doctrinal theology in the latter part of the twentieth century.

On the basis of his own research and reflection – he was an observer at the Second Vatican Council in the 1960s – Lindbeck offered an alternative definition of 'doctrine'. A Christian doctrine, Lindbeck suggested, is a social construct: it functions, successfully or unsuccessfully, as a verbal expression of the way in which Christians live. Thus, the doctrine of the Trinity is not a piece of abstract theory, but rather the expression of something fundamental to the way in which Christians worship and believe in God as Father, Son and Holy Spirit. One might give different names to those three Persons – Creator, Redeemer, Sanctifier, for example – but Lindbeck's point remains the same: they are verbal expressions of the way in which faith lives, and that is their *sole* validity and authority.

Many theologians found this a very exciting development, and the student will recognize that I was one of those who did. Lindbeck's argument seemed quite liberating: it allowed people to move away from rigid, arid definitions of what a doctrine is, towards a much more fluid appreciation of the way in which a doctrine works. Certainly, a doctrine is a limiting factor, it establishes the parameters of discussion of an issue or question. But, much more importantly, a doctrine expresses the way in which those limits and parameters are rooted in everyday life. Doctrines like those of the Church, the Eucharist, the person and work of Christ, creation: these could now be understood as vehicles for a community's specific self-definition. Doctrines were no longer definitions handed down, as if from nowhere, to be acknowledged and accepted without thought or interpretation. On the contrary, a community's doctrines were expressive of that community's *life*. Lindbeck had, it seemed, formulated a methodological tool by means of which theologians could understand how doctrines reflected the shape of belief in specific situations, and subsequently how those same doctrines, of necessity, shaped a community's theology.

And the best thing about Lindbeck's argument was that it was so obviously *right*. Doctrines are social constructs, shaped and formed by, and in, specific socio-cultural situations, as we saw with the *homoousios* clause at Nicaea. Power and authority, after all, are very practical matters, indicative of the relationships and tensions prevalent in a given situation. Small wonder, then, that the words and expressions deriving from that power and authority – doctrine – should mirror those relationships and tensions. The *nature* of doctrine, consequently, could not be something established incontrovertibly and forever. Rather, it was something in a constant state of flux and change, just as Christianity as a religion was in a constant state of flux and change.

This much, concluded Lindbeck, was good common sense, with important implications for the way in which theology should address ethical questions, because it means that the answers to such questions are to be found in the relationship between Christianity's truth claims and the social contexts in which those truth claims are made. Judgement, consequently, becomes not at all a matter of imposing a single doctrinal statement upon all situations, as one sees, for example, in some responses to the question of abortion, but rather of assessing how Christian teaching on a given subject is as much shaped by the beliefs and prejudices of its audience as it is by 'the truth'. And when judgement is understood in this way, then ethical questions can be addressed on their own terms – that is, as matters of social practice and acceptability. A good example of this is the Christian understanding of homosexuality, and whether or not God's will for life can be realized by homosexual couples in loving relationships. Whatever one's response to that question, one cannot deny that the doctrinal argument is intimately involved with matters of social practice.

There are two questions which must be put to Lindbeck's argument, however, which are very important for this chapter's discussion of doctrine. I do not say that these are *problems* for Lindbeck's position: questions are not problems, and the student should be aware by now that I do not want to encourage unnecessary attacks on significant ideas. Rather, they are things which students should think about as they attempt to test Lindbeck's hypothesis in their own study of this subject.

First, there is what one might call 'Pilate's question' (after John 18: 38), the question of truth; that is, is such and such a doctrine *true*? For example, is the doctrine of the two natures of Jesus Christ true? Or the doctrine of the Trinity? Or the *homoousios* doctrine? Certainly, one answer to this question is: 'They are true for faith'; but this is hardly adequate. A more philosophically respectable position is to ask, again with Pilate, 'What is truth?' But this too runs into immediate difficulties, because it is impossible to identify a position from which one might verify or falsify, once and for all, whether or not, for example, the doctrine of the Trinity is *true*. What this question really means, of course, is, 'Is the doctrine of the Trinity *accurate*?' – a very different matter, and one I will return to in the next section.

Lindbeck's response to this question is entirely honest: he admits that there is no possibility of verifying a specific doctrine *as true*, but instead offers two alternatives. Either one can 'bracket' the question of truth, to use a philosophical term, leaving it on one side and operating solely within methodological constraints – which turns theology into something rather like sociology. Or one can concern oneself with truth, but accept that 'truth' is itself contextual, and therefore determined for a given community by a given set of circumstances. Lindbeck prefers this latter alternative, and I too would urge students to consider its attractions. But one must be equally candid about its limitations: it is not talking about truth in any *supernatural* sense; that is, as something which is true 'out there', where God 'dwells', rather than 'in here', where we live. Truth as something contextual is an intellectually honourable argument. But it does little to answer the burning questions which many believers ask about the ultimate reality of God and the world.

The second question arises if one accepts Lindbeck's central argument, and goes something like this: when is a doctrine not a doctrine? Or better, how can one guarantee that what one thinks are one's doctrines, actually are one's doctrines? If doctrines are social constructs, then it follows logically that the way in which people live socially, as Christians in community, will constitute their 'doctrines', even if they are not made explicit. For example, on Lindbeck's definition, it was clearly a doctrine of the South African Reformed Church that Jesus Christ advocated apartheid; but no sane Christian would agree to that position, or would regard it as a valid argument. Similarly, given the events of the Holocaust during the Second World War, there is good reason to argue that anti-Semitism was a central doctrine of the German Christian Movement in Germany, indeed one of its primary doctrines; but theologians are squeamish about acknowledging this. Again, the denial of human rights to African-Americans was often central to the stance and teaching of certain Christian denominations in the United States, even if unarticulated as such. The question which arises from Lindbeck's definition, consequently, centres upon the *endorsement* or otherwise of certain beliefs and practices as doctrines: how do we endorse what we approve of and reject what we do not, given that both are equally socially constructed?

Lindbeck's answer is quite equivocal: he argues that there is a difference between *doctrines* – which are thought about and written down, and which therefore have to be *consciously* endorsed – and straightforwardly social practices, which may implicitly be relevant, but which are not ecclesial teaching. Lindbeck acknowledges that this still leaves room for difficulty, but argues that *some* such difficulty is simply constitutive of doing doctrinal theology – a disappointingly wooden final position.

The problem here for theology – and it *is* a problem – is how to speak of doctrines as the shape of theology in such a way that they both reflect the pressures and circumstances of a specific socio-cultural situation – the concern of chapter 6 – *and* pay sufficient heed to the meaning and intent of Christian history and tradition, as it has been handed down over nearly 2,000 years – the concern of chapter 5. This is the tense relationship which theology has to live with – which it does by speaking in terms of analogies and models.

3   Openness and closure

As I have said, 'analogy' means reasoning from approximately parallel cases, using one relevant situation to make sense of another. An obvious illustration is the doctrine of the Trinity, and how its language of three Persons is often interpreted via language concerning human personality and relationship. Indeed, theology in general is an excellent example of an analogical discipline, simply because its subject matter – God – is not accessible for examination and discussion in the same way that, say, the subject matter of geology or carpentry is. Theology *must* reason from parallel cases, because it cannot reason from the thing itself; this much is axiomatic. Thus the statement 'God is love' is intelligible only because we have certain ideas about what *human* love is, without which divine love would remain entirely opaque.

What does this mean for the nature of Christian doctrine? It means that doctrines cannot be propositionally true or correct; they cannot simply describe something accurately and objectively. Instead, they are arguments constructed analogically by people as they seek to understand God's relationship with the world, and more specifically that relationship as it is revealed in Jesus Christ. It is not very helpful, consequently, to think of doctrines as *analogies*; for what one is really interested in is *reasoning analogically*: that is, a way of thinking and arguing, rather than arguments as such. Doctrines, then, are arguments which arise when people think analogically about God – so doctrines like those of the Trinity, the two natures of Jesus Christ and the homoousios, are products of just such analogical reflection. It is quite simple: doctrines *exist* within arguments, even if those arguments are social constructs, and even if they are recognizable only implicitly.

Acknowledging this point, it is possible to give doctrine a more precise definition. A doctrine is a *model*. Generally in theology, models are made up of words and sentences; they are verbal arguments. The creeds of the early Church are obvious theological models, constructed by analogical reasoning about God. But one can also recognize other models of God, which, on Lindbeck's argument, are equally doctrinal: they would include human actions, relationships, works of art, liturgies – any social construction which formulates the beliefs of a given group or community. This definition allows one to encompass both what one might call traditional doctrine – the Trinity, the Incarnation, cross, resurrection and so on – and much more progressive or unsuspected doctrine – religious pop songs, for example, or religious customs. The point is that people everywhere construct models of God, in very many different forms; and when they do, whether they know it or not, they are reasoning and arguing analogically about God. (Of course, they may not think they are reasoning analogically; they may think they are describing God quite accurately and objectively. But it is very important that the student recognize that *this is not possible*, and that the reason why it is not possible is because God – reasoning theistically for the moment – is *not of the world*, and therefore cannot be described.)

Once understood and accepted, this is a wonderful activity for the theologian to be engaged in – constructing models of God! Analogically! It all sounds very creative, and so it is. And so it was back in the early Church, when councils of Christians met to decide what was to be included in orthodox Christianity, and what not. But referring back to the early Church in this way also tells us something more. It tells us that the practical implications of creating models of God include openness versus closure, inclusion versus exclusion; such activity involves establishing parameters and limits, because that is what a doctrine *does*, albeit very creatively. We can illustrate this if we stop for a moment to consider the Christian tradition in the light of our definition of doctrine.

As I argued in chapter 5, the Christian tradition is amorphous, and includes a very diverse range of characters, movements, ideas, and so on. At the same time, the central group of core

Christian doctrines – those relating to Jesus Christ, such as the Incarnation, cross and resurrection; the nature of God, such as the Trinity, creation and the Holy Spirit; and the Christian life, such as the Church and sacraments – has remained more or less constant for over 1,500 years, and in some cases even longer. Granted that the Christian tradition is full of the most astonishing models and interpretations of God and God's relationship with the world, the same core ideas and beliefs nevertheless keep on recurring.

This illustrates the paradox which I want to highlight at this point. For all the astonishing diversity and openness of Christian models of God, there is a *closure* of certain key ideas and models – doctrines – which are key, not because they are demonstrably accurate and correct, but because they successfully communicate something of the essence of the Christian faith. They thus sustain a wide range of different interpretations, and outlast other models, because they are integral to the way in which Christians *live*. If one speaks of the openness and closure of doctrine not theoretically, as if doctrines were simply concepts, but practically – like Lindbeck – it is because they arise from the real worlds in which people live. And the point I want to make is that the test of time demonstrates that certain doctrines are much more practical than others, over a much wider range of circumstances.

Now, I do not want to stretch this point further than it will happily go. There is no absolute distinction between 'open' and 'closed' doctrine, just as there is no basis on which one can state categorically which doctrines will remain vital in the developing Christian tradition (which of course is *still* developing). Similarly, there is no a priori reason why one model works and another does not. All I am offering here is a working hypothesis: students should think about the openness and closure of doctrine and models of God for themselves, as they go about the business of interpreting the Christian faith in relation to specific situations. As I have said previously, theology is an applied science, which means that the results of interpretation will become apparent only as students engage in it. A good example of this would be the doctrine of no sex before marriage, one taught by many denominations, but increasingly challenged by the specific practices of many young Christians. In such a situation, this doctrine may need to undergo considerable change and development, perhaps leading to its rejection; but that is for the interpreter to decide in the practice of interpretation.

The flexibility of this discussion of doctrine can therefore work both ways. For the more conservative, it offers a clearly defined list of closed doctrines, settled by over 1,500 years of tradition, and expressed formally in various creeds. For the more progressive, however, the openness of doctrine is a challenge and a promise: that the Christian gospel speaks in many different ways to many different situations. One can illustrate both tendencies from the history solely of modern theology: individuals like Karl Barth and Karl Rahner were quite conservative doctrinally, as even a cursory examination of the *Church Dogmatics* or *Theological Investigations* demonstrates. But more contemporary theologians, like the feminist writers Rosemary Radford Ruether and Sallie McFague – whose most recent book, *The Body of God: An Ecological Theology*, is a good example – are seemingly much more progressive in their language and argument. Perhaps the best solution is to be both conservative *and* progressive, in the best sense of both words. After all, if one is genuinely a Christian, one can hardly not conserve the economy of revelation in one's theology – Jesus Christ – and if one is genuinely practical, it is hard not to be progressive.

All this might seem unduly daunting to the beginning student, confronted by an array of theological books, each discussing a wide range of different doctrines and arguments. But there is no need to be daunted: studying theology, like studying anything else, is a cumulative process, and the position I have just been describing is quite an advanced one. Students will undoubtedly begin by considering the standard doctrines of the Christian faith in as systematic a fashion as possible, gaining knowledge of their history and traditional operation before attempting to be more adventurous. Such an approach makes good sense, and chapter 9 is intended to help at that stage (just as chapter 10 is intended to introduce the student to a wide range of progressive theological models). Some students will want to stop at this point, acquiring knowledge of the discipline and how it works. More, however, will want to go on and consider the *task* of theology, which is to interpret doctrine, and even go on to *do* theology themselves.

Doing theology in this sense is the subject matter of the next chapter, but I want to make some introductory remarks at this stage.

Simply stated, interpretation is a process of application, as I described above. Thus, if I want to interpret the doctrine of the Trinity, I have to apply it to the situation in which I live and work. More profoundly, however, interpretation is a process of engagement, between explicitly theological ideas and motifs and ideas and motifs of society and culture, politics and economics. Again, taking the Trinity as an example, engaging the Trinity with social and cultural ideas and motifs might lead me to think of scientific arguments – that three is the most stable number (as in a tripod or a three-legged stool) – or human psychology – that persons in relationship need ideally to demonstrate certain qualities (as in a non-hierarchical community). Unsurprisingly, both these approaches have been employed in interpreting the doctrine of the Trinity: the former is a staple of natural theology, and the latter was the basis of Leonardo Boff's celebrated book *Trinity and Society*.

Even if one is quite conservative in one's doctrinal position, the process of interpretation involves one in relating one's ideas and motifs to those of other people in other situations – unless one is simply in the business of dictatorially imposing one's views on others irrespective of where they stand, which should not be any theologian's position. The task of the theologian, consequently, is to be Janus-faced: to look at both text (doctrine) and context. At the interface of these, interpretation occurs, which is what I want to discuss in the next chapter.

- Christian doctrine arises from the interpretation of theology's resources: language and experience, the Bible, history and tradition, society and culture. But doctrine became the shape of theology by itself being shaped by the Church.
- The Church is therefore the authority by which doctrine is confessed; but the Church, too, is constrained by its socio-linguistic contextuality. Thus doctrines are socio-linguistic phenomena, as open to hermeneutic principles as are other such phenomena. This is illustrated by the history of doctrinal theology.
- The qualities of openness which the theologian requires, therefore, come into tense relationship with the authority as closure of the Church – at which point much theological activity occurs. In this way contemporary theology is constantly being tested in its Christian religious context – informed by the resources discussed previously.

8

Interpretation: The Task of Christian Theology

- Definition of interpretation as the task of theology by analogy with its role in other discourses, e.g. social and cultural
- Consideration of how theological interpretation works, developing themes introduced and discussed in chapter 2. Illustration of the task of theology by reference to interpretation of the Bible and tradition
- Implications of interpretation: construction of theological models according to the principles of theology as pluralistic, limited, applied, critical, constructive, imaginative
- Examination of the loci of theology in society and culture

If Part I answered the question of *how* theology speaks of God, and Part II answered the question of *what* theology works with, then Part III has been answering the *why* question: why does theology seek to speak about God at all? The short answer to this question – 'Because theology has a responsibility to reflect upon the Christian faith in order to understand it' – is sufficient as a starting point. But when a student is confronted by the bewildering variety of differing theologies, books, statements and arguments which abound in the modern world, confusion can rapidly set in. What is required, consequently, is a *general theory* of how theology sets out to answer the *why* question, what is involved in this process, what the implications of this procedure are for the way in which one understands the task of theology, and where, ultimately, one finds this task being undertaken. These are the various matters which the present chapter addresses.

To say, therefore, that interpretation is the task of theology is to say, implicitly, that interpretation addresses the initial considerations that concern theology, and that it also addresses the building blocks, the resources and responsibilities, which any good theology must have in order to function within a religious context. Thus, interpretation as a task is something which we must define carefully and test in action, to see if it is up to the stresses which the contemporary situation places on it. We must consider how well interpretation channels the important questions of history and tradition; how it makes sense of, and employs, language and experience; how, of utmost significance, it relates theology to the Bible; and how, of most immediate relevance, interpretation addresses the very considerable issues which society and culture raise, and which theology must resolve if it is to move away from being simply theoretical, towards being practical and thereby *useful*.

In what follows, I intend to move to a new level in this introduction to theology. Having established the necessary parameters of theology as a working discipline, and defined the specific areas in which it seeks to operate, I will now consider the questions of how one becomes involved in and with theological argument. With the tools under our belts, we are now moving on to consider how they can be used to produce theological models. Those models will be shaped by the doctrines which I considered in the previous chapter, as well as by the specific circumstances in which the theologians constructing the models find themselves. As such models will, initially at least, be the most immediate thing to confront the student, however, it is well that we approach them on the basis of a secure understanding of their *origin*. There is nothing inherently difficult about understanding theological models. But their sheer variety can confound if they are not handled carefully and, yes, interpreted.

1 What is interpretation?

The first thing to assert about interpretation is that everyone does it, even if they do not realize it. It is part of the business of reading, and entails discovering meaning in a text from one's own point of view. For example, when one picks up a newspaper and reads about a natural disaster in Africa or some other stricken part of the world, one does not simply take in the information contained in the report (unless one is a walking computer, incapable of compassion). Rather, one *responds* to what one reads: it finds meaning and resonance in one's own experience, which in turn generates reflection, action, emotion, indifference or whatever, depending upon what sort of person one is and how involved one becomes in the particular story. The same thing can be seen in television sports programmes, where one might witness someone hitting a home run, or winning Wimbledon, or riding a Derby winner, and one interprets what one sees according to how one responds to the information and images one is absorbing. *The New York Times* has on its masthead 'All the News that's Fit to Print' – but even to say this entails interpretation.

These are very ordinary examples of interpretation, and one can draw more sophisticated instances from the world of the arts. For example, ballet, opera, theatre and the concert hall (rock or classical) all involve the audience in the business of interpretation: one watches an opera or play, following the action and responding according to the meaning that one finds in the opera or play itself. Some people find Puccini's *Madame Butterfly* so traumatic that they leave the opera house in floods of tears. Others are entirely unmoved, preferring a play by Arthur Miller. Still others respond most immediately to rock music, be it contemporary or of slightly older vintage. In all cases, however, interpretation is at the heart of how we perceive and appreciate the things we witness and experience in the world. This is not a mysterious thing, or even something which requires a great deal of thought. It is simply one big part of being human, of living in a particular situation and responding to the different texts, events and experiences within it.

Obviously, a great deal of this interpretation goes on without one realizing it. If one is watching a *Tom and Jerry* cartoon, for example, one does not sit there dissecting its story and meaning in order to further one's understanding of popular culture. On the contrary, meaning is generally encountered and generated through the unreflective acceptance of common cultural norms and patterns. One accepts what everyone else accepts, so that a fund of what one might call 'social meaning' is communicated via many different media. In large part this is how democracy works in the Western world. Some would call it apathy, but on the whole it is successful, because people are social and like to feel part of a community which *agrees* about certain things.

One can recognize this phenomenon in a society like Britain or the United States, where popular devotion to certain hymns and carols means that they are repeated again and again all over the country, irrespective of denominational distinctions. Certainly, they are successful partly – perhaps largely – because they are actually good. But at the same time, many hymns are repeated again and again and again simply because they have become symbols of popular faith and piety. Everyone knows and loves 'Silent Night' because, well . . . it's 'Silent Night'. In this way we see how interpretation often follows the accepted, and acceptable, norms of society and culture. Again, this is simply part of the normal rhythms of living socially with other people.

In theology these pressures from society and culture are every bit as present as anywhere else, and theology must be aware of them. At the same time, there is also theology's responsibility to history, tradition and the Bible, which means that interpretation has to be undertaken with more reflection, and more seriousness, than it sometimes receives in other, more informal contexts. Because interpretation is the specific *task* of theology, theology must take interpretation very seriously indeed. It must appreciate and understand as fully as possible what it means to interpret a text, or a historical event or a story about Jesus Christ in the New Testament. It must demonstrate this seriousness because it *matters* what interpretations theology generates – it matters what meaning theology assigns to texts, events and experiences.

Why is this the case? Simply because the meaning which theology generates carries with it power and authority. It influences people, and whenever one influences someone else, great responsibility thereby ensues, recognized or not. When, for example, a theologian argues that the story of Pentecost (Acts 2) has 'such-and-such' a meaning rather than any other – for example, that the Holy Spirit is now present in the world – he or she is giving that particular reading a significance in the eyes of his or her audience which may change the way in which individuals think about themselves, their church, and their faith. Theologians must, therefore, engage in interpretation with considerable care and restraint, because interpretation, at heart, acts as the junction through which the widest variety of ideas and situations receive meaning and significance. This is a point I made earlier in the book in referring to Stanley Hauerwas's arguments against war, from a position of confessed pacifism: stating arguments, making an interpretation, has implications which one must acknowledge, as Hauerwas does.

This itself implies that interpretation can be a dangerous thing, which is certainly the case if by 'dangerous' one means risky. Interpretation, particularly in theology, is generally well-intentioned. But because it acts to bring together such disparate things as society and culture, history and tradition, language and experience, and because it can be viewed from as many different perspectives as there are people to interpret, interpretation itself needs to be controlled; it needs certain methodological parameters, beyond which it cannot go. Why? Because one cannot say that anything goes; because the faith and the tradition *must* militate against the improper appropriation of Christian beliefs and symbols. We have already seen one example of this, the South African Dutch Reformed Church, and the evil which a group can become party to when it does not observe limitations upon its theology.

Despite the fact that interpretation is by definition something which can occur in many different ways, reflecting the plurality of theologies which themselves are contingent upon a wide plurality of historical contexts, there are certain things which interpretation *should* do, and certain things it should *not* do, if it is to be faithful to the considerations and responsibilities which I spent the first half of this book elaborating. This means that we must now go on to consider how theology goes about the business of *interpreting*.

2 How does interpretation work?

Again, there is a simple answer which one can offer as a way of approaching the question: namely, that interpretation works by engaging the world of the text in question with the world of the reader, in order to generate meaning. More philosophically, this discipline is called hermeneutics, or the theory of interpretation, a technical word which derives originally from the name of the Greek god Hermes, the winged-heeled messenger, itself a graphic example of the way in which interpretation 'carries' meaning from text to reader and back again. Interpretation is something which works two ways, changing both the meaning of a text, as people read it from different perspectives, and the readers themselves, as their attitudes and actions are altered by what they find in specific texts. Again, think of *The New York Times*: 'All the News that's Fit to Print'. That statement affects both the reader and the publisher, and is a good example of the process I am discussing.

There is a danger that this idea will appear more difficult than it really is, because what I am trying to identify here is the *flexibility* of interpretation, through which meaning is communicated not in some dead manner, but as a living, vital force, possessing the power to change both how we perceive and understand texts and how we perceive and understand our own lives. Consider, for example, Charles Dickens's novel *A Christmas Carol*, which everyone knows, and which everyone can relate to their own lives. In this sense, the meaning of Dickens's story is that people find their *own* meaning in it; that, consequently, people *learn* by reading this story, and as a result change their own lives to fulfil the high moral and social ideals which Dickens expresses. The same can be said of all Dickens's novels, which on one level can be read as attempts to educate nineteenth-century English society, but which also have meaning for contemporary society at the end of the twentieth century. The same point can be made about many American novels, such as those by Edith Wharton and Mark Twain, or more recently John Updike and Alice Walker.

Interpretation, therefore, has nothing to do with simply dissecting texts, rather as one would fillet a fish, so as to arrive at *the* meaning of a particular book or event or experience, which can then be perfectly communicated to whoever cares to listen. On the contrary, meaning exerts more power of its own than one at first realizes, so interpretation has to be subtle and sophisticated, flexible and sensitive, to express any meaning at all. One cannot, for example, exhaust the meaning of the Second World War simply by telling one story, even if that narrative is as long as Winston Churchill's. On the contrary, an event like the Second World War sustains many different interpretations – a quality which is shared in principle by any and every text, event and experience, small or large. Think, more recently, of the assassination of President John F. Kennedy in 1963, and the many different interpretations of 'the facts' it has generated.

At the same time, interpretation in *theology* is not simply about discovering meaning and having it change the way in which one looks at society and culture, although this is very important and often determines the effective differences between distinct theologies. Rather, interpretation in theology is channelled and guided by history and tradition, the Bible, experience and language, so that when it generates meaning, it does so within certain very clear limits: namely, doctrines. Failure to recognize these limits, a failure which occurs quite often in contemporary theology, is ultimately a failure of responsibility towards one's own theological heritage. We are all in the business of generating meaning through interpretation; this is part of what it is to be human. But in theology we generate meaning through interpretation in accordance with certain historical, traditional and ecclesial requirements. This is what makes theology *theology*, rather than humanism.

To illustrate this point, let us consider the example of Christology, the study of the person and work of Jesus Christ, taking as an example a central New Testament text, John 11: 25: 'I am the resurrection and the life; he who believes in me, though he die, yet shall he live, and whoever lives and believes in me shall never die.' Naturally, one can interpret this sentence in a number of different ways, and those ways will have a number of different outcomes in people's lives. One might, for example, find it the most inspirational of texts, full of spiritual and devotional significance. But one might just as easily think it nonsensical, or romantic delusion on a grand scale, particularly if one were inclined to question the specific content of such ideas as 'resurrection' and 'eternal life'. Whatever one's response, it illustrates the way in which interpretation generates meaning, because meaning is about appropriation and application to the world in which one lives. Meaning has a *practical* effect.

In theology, though, we cannot accept simply *any* interpretation of this passage. On the contrary, the meaning we find therein, if we are orthodox Christian theologians and if, consequently, we are attempting to say something meaningful to traditional Christian faith, will be constrained by certain historical, traditional and classical questions which help to define the boundaries within which Christology should operate. For example, the following questions *should* occur to the theologian as he or she attempts to interpret John 11: 25: is it historically true – that is, did Jesus say it in this fashion? What does the passage mean by 'resurrection' and 'life'? What does John/Jesus mean when he says that believers will never die? How was this belief/argument understood in the early Church? is it compatible with traditional Christian definitions of hope? To what extent is such hope limited to the world of the early Church? All these questions, and others, must be answered before we move on to the question of what meaning we can give to John 11: 25 from the viewpoint of contemporary society and culture. The interpretation which finally emerges, whether we realize it or not, will be influenced by a myriad of factors, far more indeed than the altogether simplistic notion of what we might think the passage means.

Interpretation, therefore, is always a frustrating business. In the interests of Christian self-definition, theologians cannot simply say whatever they like about particular texts, biblical or otherwise, without at the same time abandoning something integral to the identity of Christianity as a *historical* religion. Interpretation is a matter of relating such serious, historical questions to the immediate agendas which we encounter as soon as we, as theologians, move out into society to attempt to communicate the meaning we have discovered to the community to which we belong. In this respect, too, interpretation works rather like a road junction, through which different vehicles pass, with varying speeds and directions, but all of them important elements in the life and movement of the community in question.

Granted this general model of how theology realizes its task through interpretation, what can we say about its implications for theology as a whole? How does this understanding of the interpretative task of theology affect the way in which we understand theology as a discipline devoted to both the specifics of the Christian religion and the responsibility to say something meaningful about the world in which it operates? This raises certain important issues which need to be acknowledged before I go any further into the production of specific theological models.

3 Implications of interpretation

First, we must say that there cannot be one single way of doing theology which is valid for all times and places. We must accept that theology will be pluralistic, because its task is interpretative, and because interpretation is established in the principle of pluralism. Many people do not like this, claiming instead that the task of theology as interpretation is really to communicate the objective content of the Bible and tradition, both of which witness to God's revelation in Jesus Christ. But, as we have seen, that view founders quickly, once we start to think about meaning, how it is produced, and the people and texts it brings together. People are different, and therefore meaning is different. Interpretation should reflect these differences.

This is an important point, not because theology seeks to relegate God's revelation in Jesus Christ to a subsidiary level, where it becomes less important than what people have to say about the world in which they live, but, on the contrary, because revelation itself, as grace, is far too big a subject for any one theology to discuss satisfactorily. Pluralism in theology thus points in two directions simultaneously, thereby ensuring both recognition of the significance of the witnessing community as it struggles to live in a specific environment and recognition of the glory and majesty of God, who, by definition, transcends the limits of any one human discourse. The Word, consequently, cannot be limited by human words; but human words are themselves empowered by the Word to address their own world of experience, society and culture. This, here in devotional terms, is something central to Christian belief.

Second, therefore, the Bible, history and tradition are constrained by the twin pressures of the Word and human words, of witnessing to God's revelation in Jesus Christ – their primary meaning or sense – and also being interpreted in terms of the specific viewpoint of individual Christian churches and communities – their secondary meaning or reference. Theology, too, is constrained by these twin pressures, which means that in an important way theology today must be set alongside the Bible, history and tradition as *itself* part of the process of Christian identification, seeking to relate faith to an increasingly uncertain world. And such theology takes many forms, only one of which is academic or professional theology. Other theologies are found in plays and films, music and dance, television and radio. Why? Because theology is going on wherever people attempt to communicate something of their faith, by any one (or more) of a variety of different media.

It would be wrong, however, to imply that theology is implicated in this process to anything like the same degree that these other things are, because people do not turn to theology in anything like the same way that they turn to the Bible (for example). On the contrary, theology must accept that its role is to observe, to witness to this process as it happens, and sometimes to speak prophetically to the situations it witnesses. But, if this is to be achieved, then theology must *offer* something; it must place itself at risk, jeopardizing its apparent security for the sake of its role as witness.

How can theology undertake this risk? By entering the process of interpreting, by offering models which relate the resources and responsibilities of theology to the specific pressures and duties of the world in which it operates. In this sense, a model is a representation of certain views and opinions, informed certainly by critical reflection and Christian faith, but simultaneously limited and relativized by the fact that it is impossible to encapsulate in one model all the complexities and diversities of even the simplest social context.

What does this mean for theology? It means that theological

models can take on a number of very different forms. A model
could, for example, be a book, which is very common; such have
been in existence since the first century of the common era. (The
Fourth Gospel is just such a book of theology.) Or it could be a
letter, like one of Paul's, or a hymn, or a sermon, or an action, or
a monument to the dead, such as a cenotaph or a war memorial,
or a prayer, sometimes a silent form of theological model which
may be the most profound. Theological models do not have to
conform to certain, stereotypical patterns. Certainly, this is
generally the case, though there is much to be said for the 'big
book' of theology which asks and answers the 'big questions'
(every student will know one, with varying degrees of affection).
But new theological models occur all the time as people witness
to their dual responsibilities, to the historical religion and all
those who have gone before and to the world in which they live.
So many of the most popular hymns are such models: memorials
to a past faith which nurture present faith.

Of course, the obvious implication of all this, which must be
mentioned, is that many theological models are constructed
unconsciously by people who are entirely unaware that they are
constructing an interpretation which relates their world to that of
the Christian faith. This in turn means that there is a significant
distinction between thinking theologically, on the one hand,
which means reflecting deliberately and carefully upon the way in
which people interpret faith, the way in which such interpretations can and should be presented for discussion and further
reflection, and acting implicitly theologically, on the other hand.
Anyone can do the latter, and during their religious lives most
people and communities do so at some stage. But the former
must have a special place in both the life of the Church in general
(and individual churches in particular) and on the edge of the
Church. What do I mean? Simply that theology as a discipline
must seek a degree of independence which theological models in
themselves, as interpretations of particular contexts, cannot
possess. Hence theology's special character, and an important
qualification, which I have mentioned several times: one need not
be a Christian in order to study Christian theology, because theology entails the study of models and interpretation, rather than
faith itself – as I have reiterated, from my introduction onwards.

This brings me to the important question of *where* one finds theology, with which I shall conclude this chapter. But because this discussion has important implications for the way in which we understand theological models and their production, I want to make a few qualifying statements. First, though it stands on the edge of the Church, theology cannot claim any special authority; rather, whatever it has to offer, it offers with all humility to the witnessing community. Second, however, the absence of such authority liberates theology to adopt a *questioning* role. Thus, theology asks questions about faith and its doctrines not in order simply to serve churches, but to interpret and thereby understand the meaning of faith and its doctrines in given situations. It does this by posing questions to those doctrines and situations.

4   The locus of theology

All of this implies, quite correctly, that although theologians occupy a particular office and practise a particular discipline in relation to the Church (and it is sometimes a distant, sometimes a close, relationship), theology can also be done by anyone in any place at any time. Speaking of God is an open activity, rather than one closed off except to certain expert practitioners. It is thus quite legitimate to speak of theology occurring in churches, schools, universities, even on street corners – indeed, anywhere that people come together and, one way or another, start to speak about God in terms of the revelation which is believed to have occurred in Jesus Christ. Theology, on this model, is about communication, and interpretation is communication such as attempts to convey meaning, for a specific purpose. In theology that purpose is to understand faith: faith seeking understanding.

Developing this point somewhat, it should also be apparent that theology can occur via a number of different media. It can certainly occur as written or spoken text, as in a popular or an academic book, or a sermon or address. But it can also occur as a poem, a piece of music, an action, a relationship, a sacrament (for example, the Eucharist), a film, a play, an opera – in fact, almost anything can communicate theological meaning. And throughout the twentieth century, theology and theologians amongst others have used all these different formats to say something about belief in Jesus Christ. Examples of these categories are T. S. Eliot's *Four Quartets*; REM's song 'Losing my Religion'; Dietrich Bonhoeffer's participation in the bomb plot to assassinate Hitler in 1944; the friendship, forged in the initial interests of ecumenism, between the archbishop of Canterbury and the Pope in 1982; the celebration of the Eucharist at the reconsecration of Coventry Cathedral; Martin Scorsese's *The Last Temptation of Christ*; Andrew Lloyd-Webber's and ·Time Rice's *Jesus Christ Superstar*; and Aaron Copland's opera *The Tender Land*. In their differing ways – and not all of them would find universal acceptance – each of these says something meaningful about the Christian faith, or an aspect of it. Each communicates *something* of the meaning of God's revelation in Christ and its significance for human existence, whether from the perspective of faith itself or from that of a thorough questioning of faith.

This is very attractive: it allows theology to respond flexibly to a wide range of different emotions and situations, whilst simultaneously maintaining something important about the *origin* of faith in God. It is, moreover, something which has occurred throughout the Christian tradition: one thinks, for example, of the medieval mystery plays, or Bach's B Minor Mass, or the various texts of all descriptions which Christians have created as witnesses to their faith in God. Far from being an arid, desiccated form of intellectual reflection (although unfortunately it can be this), therefore, theology has the most colourful of languages: St Anthony of Padua preaching to the fishes *is* theology every bit as much as Karl Barth's monumental *Church Dogmatics*.

Yet being a theologian is also most importantly a very specific office; theology is a job which someone has to do, and which not everyone is capable of doing. A clear illustration of this point comes from the earliest period of the Christian Church, as recorded in the New Testament, with the contrast between the letters of Paul to the young churches and the Fourth Gospel, written by John for his community. Paul's letters contain a great deal of theology: one finds him responding to the particular circumstances and questions of his young, immature congregations, and sometimes he even gives conflicting advice, because of this contextual constraint. By contrast, the Fourth Gospel *is* theology from first to last: John gives a coherent understanding of the belief that God has acted in Jesus Christ for the judgement of the world, and that Christ is present in the Johannine community itself. John's reflection, then, is systematic: it develops a consistent argument, relating its various themes to the one central doctrine of the Incarnate Word. Paul's letters, though equally profound and meaningful, are not systematic; that luxury, perhaps, was not open to Paul as he travelled the Mediterranean world in the name of Jesus.

Being systematic: this is the quality which marks out the office of the theologian in the community, and therefore in terms of the relationship between faith and society. Naturally, not all theological statements are systematic, and, as we have seen, there are many different theological texts which are not as organized and structured as the Fourth Gospel. But here we must make a distinction between the academic theology *per se* and popular theology *per accidens*: the former is a discipline, conducted with a specific goal in mind; the latter, though perhaps goal-orientated, does not have academic theology's vested interest in being systematic.

What is the true goal of systematic theology? Within the Church, the task of systematic theology, in so far as it produces interpretative models which seek to understand faith, is to interpret *doctrine* – that is, teachings about the Christian faith – by relating faith's central elements to the world in which human beings live. Theology, therefore, is all about teaching: teaching students, perhaps, in so far as they want to understand the Christian faith in terms of their social and cultural context; but primarily teaching believers as they attempt to follow Jesus Christ, hope for the coming glory of God, and work towards the realization of God's Kingdom on earth. Where is theology, then? It is present wherever Christian teaching occurs, something recognized by every denomination as integral to the life of faith. And hence the study of theology finds a natural home almost everywhere people speak meaningfully and intelligently of their faith in God.

It should now be much clearer to the reader how the various elements of Parts I and II fit together, and how they find their natural expression in the task of theology as interpretation which I have outlined here. The qualities considered in Part I in particular are all qualities which one finds naturally enough in everyday life and society. Indeed, one might almost go as far as to say that they are qualities that theologians need to learn from the world in which they live. Similarly, the specific resources discussed in Part II are all things which people encounter generally as they go about their everyday lives. They may not do it quite as explicitly as I have done in chapters 3–6, but nevertheless they do it.

What does all this say about theology as a specific discipline, with particular responsibilities and resources and directed towards a clear goal? It says that theology, far from being a distant, academic business, fit only for universities and theological colleges, is, when properly understood, a vibrant, colourful, consuming affair, one in which very different questions and very different situations are all addressed with equal vigour and respect. Understanding theology in this way brings it back directly into the very heart of the way people live their lives. No one can avoid the questions of theology, whether they are believers, agnostics or atheists, because the *stuff* of theology is the very essence of life itself.

That said, theology has also to come down to earth; it has, therefore, to recognize that this apparent freedom is also constrained by the urgent needs of the Church as it seeks to witness to its faith and its gifts in an often alien, hostile world. This is a situation which has confronted Christian theologians since the time of Paul and John, and it is a situation which has resulted, overwhelmingly, in the same kind of response: the production of doctrine, along certain recurring lines of enquiry. This forms the subject matter of chapter 9.

- Interpretation is a very common skill: the vast majority of people practise it constantly in their daily lives. Identifying it as the task of theology is therefore establishing theology as an intensely practical discipline, whose basic skill is familiar to all.
- Interpretation works by constructing models: again, people do this constantly in their daily lives. Theology's models are informed by its resources, particularly the Bible and tradition; but they are still analogous to other social and cultural forms.
- The implications of model building return theology to its origins in the principles of chapter 2: theology is pluralistic, limited, etc., because interpretative models are pluralistic, etc.
- Theology is far more ubiquitous than people commonly realize: theology is to be found wherever people reflect upon their life by reference to a religious conviction, however subconscious this process might be. Theology thus cannot be consigned to the ghetto: it requires location in the everyday world.

PART IV
Looking Around, Past and Present

Acquiring the key skill, interpretation, is the most important part of the student's theological education; that, and constant practice. What remains is to read, write, think and discuss theology, developing the skills of Part III on the resources and responsibilities of Part II, ever mindful of the qualities and relationships of Part I. All I want to do in Part IV, consequently, is to assist this process by outlining some of the key areas of past theologies and the dominant motifs of contemporary ones. Chapters 9 and 10 mirror chapters 7 and 8, so recurrent themes focus upon Christianity's central doctrines, and contemporary issues relate directly to the way in which interpretation is practised today.

In chapter 9 I discuss certain classical doctrines, problems and situations which students will encounter as they learn and think more about theology's past. They are all fairly obvious, and many of them have been discussed, or hinted at, in previous chapters. What I want to do here is make their treatment explicit, to give the student a good idea of the state of play in the discipline's past. Larger, more data-based textbooks will help students with background information, so that they acquire a good knowledge by channelling their efforts along the lines suggested here (see Suggestions for Further Reading). Chapter 9 is therefore straightforwardly pedagogical: all I have in mind is a map of some of the landmarks which students will encounter as they study theology.

Chapter 10 follows a similar brief, with the proviso that in it I consider contemporary issues, focusing in particular upon the currently tense relationship between issues and ideas, reading the available literature, and some possible future trends and developments. As regards the first, I extol the virtue of remaining theoretical while attending to practical matters, sure in the conviction that theory is an intensely practical activity. Second, I offer a short guide to the myriad byways of primary and secondary literature, where so many find difficulties when it comes to studying contemporary theology. And regarding the third, I outline what I think will be major issues over the next twenty years of Christian theology. These suggestions are by no means exhaustive, and are fairly predictable; but they are important. By this stage, the student should be able to think through the significance of an issue like human sexuality in contemporary theology, understanding the demands it places both upon traditional and biblical doctrine and upon the ability of theologians to relate such ideas to their contemporary situations.

9

Recurrent Themes in Christian Theology

- Classical doctrines: the Incarnation, cross, resurrection, ascension, creation, Trinity, Holy Spirit, Church, sacraments
- Classical problems: Christianity's historical origins, choice of analogy, eschatology, Christianity's relations with other religions
- Classical situations: the levels of theological activity, liberation from power and oppression, secularism, philosophy, relationship between society and individual

By this stage, if the student has been reading imaginatively and following up some of the suggested reading, he or she will have a good working knowledge and understanding of the discipline of theology, its principal areas (and how they relate to other, associated disciplines) and, most importantly, how it works. That was the explicit concern of the last chapter, which focused on the question of interpretation. But I am aware that, just as the discussion reaches the most exciting and creative stage, so it becomes most daunting, because interpreting doctrine, the 'stuff' of theology, induces in most theologians – teachers and students alike – a profound anxiety. It is at this point that everyone needs help, and that some guidance as regards the present situation in theology becomes most useful. That is what I am going to provide in the two chapters of this final section.

Going a bit deeper into this issue, I want to state quite explicitly that doing theology is fundamentally a difficult thing; there is no point in denying this. It involves a way of relating to the material one is working with and the specific practical situation within which one is operating, which is difficult to acquire. Yet, at the same time, *studying* theology is comparatively straightforward, for one very good reason: people have been doing theology, more or less in the same fashion, for nearly 2,000 years. Though certain philosophical presuppositions have altered – for example, most theologians do not have an Aristotelian understanding of the physical world any more, as St Thomas Aquinas did – the central agenda of Christian theology has remained the same. Students can look at the work of Augustine, or Aquinas, or Martin Luther, or Karl Barth, or Jürgen Moltmann, and recognize a strong degree of resemblance. It is only when one comes to the most recent theologies that this picture starts to alter significantly, though even now, there are still many theologians operating within the time-honoured, easily recognizable framework.

This reassuring picture is the subject matter of the present chapter; I will consider the more challenging of the contemporary developments in chapter 10. What I want to discuss now, though, are the classical doctrines, problems and situations which recur in Christian theology, and which any student looking at its history, particularly its modern history, will encounter again and again. As always, given my cumulative way of discussing theology, I presuppose the student's familiarity with the subject matter of the previous chapters: namely, the interpretative character of theology and the construction and discussion of theological models on the basis of analogy. Against this background I will discuss some classical doctrines, classical problems and classical situations. There is not space to discuss these things in detail, admittedly. But by thinking about the issues involved as creatively as possible, and following up the themes via the Suggestions for Further Reading, the student will gain a thorough understanding of the shape of classical Christian theology.

1   Classical doctrines

The Incarnation, cross, resurrection, ascension, creation, Trinity, Holy Spirit, Church, sacraments: this is not an exhaustive list, but these are the central teachings of Christianity, and by considering their history, development and expression, the student will gain knowledge of the recurring themes of theology. By concentrating upon these doctrines, consequently, I am making a pragmatic as well as a theological point: these are the central questions which students of Christian theology need to consider, and are the central doctrines covered by the theological literature.

At first glance these doctrines seem very disparate, so the student can be forgiven for asking, 'how are they related to each other?' But the answer to this question is of course fundamental to the discipline as a whole. They are related because they all converge on the same historical individual, Jesus of Nazareth, and because they all attempt to make some sense of his life on earth, his relationship with God and his significance for humanity. Thus, the Incarnation, cross, resurrection and ascension all originate in the New Testament, more specifically in the gospel narratives; whatever the later traditional development, the roots of these ideas lie at the very origins of the historical faith. Similarly, the doctrines of the Trinity and the Holy Spirit, although they seem quite distant from historical considerations, are ways of understanding Jesus' relationship with God: the Trinity, as we have seen, is a model for understanding the relations between Father, Son and Holy Spirit; and the Holy Spirit is for Christianity the presence of God in the world as Person, sent by Jesus Christ. Finally, the doctrines of creation, Church and the sacraments all point towards beliefs held because the thing concerned is understood by reference to Christ – as in the Christian understanding of creation, which states that the world was created through the Son of God – or because Christ himself instituted the specific office – like the Church and the sacraments. This is the first, most important point for students to understand: that Christian doctrines all relate to Jesus of Nazareth in some way.

The task of the student of theology, then, is to interpret how these Jesus-related doctrines have meaning in their given situation, which involves two important aspects of the same interpretative process. First, students must ask the question of how a given doctrine originates in the economic revelation of God in the world – that is, in the actual, physical life of Jesus of Nazareth nearly 2,000 years ago. Second, they must ask how a given doctrine shows something about God's immanent being – that is, how God is in Godself. As these are crucial ideas, I will explore them more fully by discussing the example of the Trinity. Why the doctrine of the Trinity? Because it is a doctrine about the Persons of God, their relationships and love – all themes which are at least intelligible to most people.

As I have already argued, the doctrine of the Trinity is a model, consisting of a series of propositions about God's being, made by analogy with human existence. The question of **economy**, in relation to the Trinity, thus asks how this model of God's being relates to the historical life of Jesus of Nazareth. The answer is as follows. As far as we can tell from the gospels, Jesus' mission and message were dominated by perceived relationships between three 'Persons': the Father, the Son and the Holy Spirit. Granted that the evidence for this assertion is contained in documents in the New Testament which are themselves interpretations of original events, nevertheless, on this matter we are as certain as we can be about anything in Christian origins: Jesus spoke of Father, Son and Holy Spirit. Hence, the epistemological grounds upon which theology speaks of the Trinity are to be found – axiomatically – in the narratives of the historical Jesus. How those narratives were then developed by subsequent generations is the story of tradition.

The **immanence** question in theology is equally straight-forward, once certain moves are made. The first is again axiomatic: one cannot speak directly of God's immanent being; therefore any such speech must be by way of analogy. It makes certain claims – which are confessed, not demonstrated – about God's being by analogy with human being, specifically on the basis of one human being, Jesus of Nazareth. Thus, when theologians make significant claims for the doctrine of the Trinity – for example, that God is three-in-one, co-equal, co-eternal, or that the three Persons are engaged in eternal mutual embrace/love/identity/will – they are not describing God's being. Rather, they are creating images, models, by analogy with human being, of what they think God is like because of what God reveals of Godself in Jesus Christ. This should make the student realize that in theology talk of the immanent Trinity can occur only as talk of the economic Trinity – for that is the only way in which Christian theology knows God.

In fact, this relationship between the economic and the immanent recurs throughout Christian doctrine, so much so that one
can speak of a golden rule: one speaks of something as being of
God – immanent – because, and in so far as, one speaks of something being revealed by God – economically – in Jesus Christ.
Here again I can point to the shape of Christian doctrine as being
Christlike: theological epistemology – the good reasons why theologians think they know and understand certain things – begins
with Jesus of Nazareth. It may take the form of biblical theology,
where valid ideas and motifs are drawn from the biblical witness.
Or it may be something apparently different, such as traditional
systematic theology's development of original ideas and motifs in
creative engagement with that theology's specific situation. But
the point remains the same: Jesus Christ is the unavoidable origin
of Christian doctrine, an argument which, because it is centred
upon a human being, has important ethical implications for how
theologies speak of other human beings.

Some theologies, though not rejecting this position, try to sup-
plement it by reference to other possible avenues: for example,
natural theology, which itself takes several forms. Thus, a theologian like the Swiss Emil Brunner argued that one can become
aware of God's existence by being in tune with creation, because
creation – in the guise of a waterfall, or a newborn baby, or a
beautiful sunset – indirectly mirrors God's being. Or, like Hans
Urs von Balthasar, one might argue that the glories of European
high culture – Grünewald's Isenheim altar-piece, Bach's *St
Matthew Passion*, or the Sistine Chapel in Rome – themselves
reflect, however mysteriously, the glory of the Lord. Or, like
Friedrich Schleiermacher, one might argue that constitutive of
human being itself is the intuitive ability to 'sense and taste the
Infinite', to be aware of God's presence in the world. Or, similar
to Schleiermacher, one might, like Karl Rahner, argue that
human existence is implicitly religious, in terms of the way in
which humans know and understand things (like their own mor-
tality and limitation). Each of these natural theologies adds something to a more straightforward theology of the Word – one
focusing exclusively upon Jesus Christ. But at no point do any of
these four theologians supplant Word theology with any other
kind. Christian theology does not supplant Christ.

When reading about the recurring themes of Christian doctrine, therefore, students will encounter a wide variety of different ideas and material, much of which is useful and meaningful,
some of which is not. And they will have to evaluate and interpret those ideas and material from the point of view of their own
specific situation. What is important, however, is not what one
says, so much as how one says it. Remember the useful maxim
'There is nothing new under the sun': so much has been said and
written over the last 2,000 years that it is highly unlikely that any
theologian or student will ever say anything original on these
topics. But this does not mean that originality is not possible in
the course of interpreting central themes in a given time and
place. The best theologians and students realize this instinctively,
and the best theologies are not those which attempt to say new
and radical things, but rather those which seek to address the
Christian faith anew in their own situations. There is an important distinction between 'new' and 'anew' which lies at the heart
of Christian theology.

With these thoughts on the economic and the immanent, the
student is equipped with a central distinction which runs
throughout the classical doctrines of the Christian faith and their
interpretation: wherever the student turns, he or she should be
able to detect, somewhere, this relationship at work. But this
working distinction, which is so important methodologically,
does not solve every difficulty. It simply provides a vital tool in
thinking through the classical problems which theology always
encounters. I want to turn to some of these now.

2   Classical problems

Again, I make no claims here to be offering an exhaustive
account of Christian theology's 'classical problems'. That is
beyond even the largest textbook, and in any case there is seldom
much explicit agreement on what exactly such problems are. To
some degree, consequently, I am on virgin territory at this point.
But I hope and expect that people will agree when I say that the
following are indeed classically problematic for Christian theology: Christianity's historical origins, choice of analogy, eschato-

logy, and its relationships with other religions. I will consider each separately.

In the previous section I talked about God's economic revelation as taking place in Jesus of Nazareth, and said that this constitutes Christianity's primary theological epistemology. This implies that the question of Christianity's historical origins is fundamental to one's understanding of the Christian economy. But this does not mean that theology here appeals to historical facts and data. On the contrary, history is itself a process of interpretation – which in turn means, significantly, that the problem of historical origins in Christian theology is itself a problem of interpretation rather than of archaeological research. This is so important that I will say it as simply as possible: theology is not interested in the historical facts about its origins in Jesus Christ.

Why is this the case? Because there is no point of view from which one can either verify or falsify the claims which theologians make about the historical origins of Christianity. One might, for example, want to make the Sermon on the Mount fundamental to one's theology, incorporating it into one's model of God's ethical command to humanity – as many theologians do. But, like it or not, there are no sound epistemological grounds for regarding the pristine delivery of the Sermon as we now have it as incontrovertible fact. Leaving aside the obvious difficulties concerning its record and transmission, there is still this most significant problem: how do we know what we think we know? The answer is simple, as I have argued several times: theology does not begin with facts; it begins with axioms, which allow of no demonstration. For better or for worse, it is axiomatic and therefore interpretative for Christian theology that (in this case) Jesus' Sermon on the Mount reveals God's will. As historical origin, therefore, it is interpreted historical origin.

This, of course, is a restriction upon theology, and rightly so. Theology is in the business of interpreting doctrine, which requires considerable creativity and imagination, application and encounter. If theology could be reduced to brute data, then obviously it would not require this significant human input. It would then become something like archaeology, rather than theology: the science of beginnings, not of God. Biblical archaeology is a fascinating and honourable discipline in its own right. But it is not theology.

The problem of which analogy starts from a similar point. In Christian theology such use of analogy has a long and distinguished heritage, unsurprisingly: after all, since it is axiomatic for such theology that God is not objectively present in the world, it must also be axiomatic that theology speaks of God by drawing approximate parallels between the way people exist and what theology wants to say about God. Such analogical reasoning goes back to Plato and Aristotle in the Greek philosophical tradition, and became pre-eminent in Christian theology (though it was always present) in the work of Thomas Aquinas. It has two major strands, which, to give them their technical Latin names, are the *analogia entis* and the *analogia fidei*. I will define these separately.

The *analogia entis* is the analogy of being, talking about God's being on the basis of certain observed, reasoned claims about human being. For example, the claim that 'God is love' – though it is of course also biblical (see 1 John 4: 16) – is an analogical statement about being: because love is regarded as one of the highest human qualities, it is predicated of God's being by a process of parallel reasoning. Similarly, theologians speak of God as having relationships and as encountering people in the midst of their lives – again, examples of the *analogia entis* at work. Supplementary to a biblical theology, which seeks authority in the original Christian texts, the use of the *analogia entis* is an example of natural theology, talking about God by talking about the world. Fundamental to so much natural theology, and so much use of the *analogia entis*, is the argument that because God is creator and the world is God's creation, then one can perceive in the world, however incompletely and indirectly, the shadow or trace of God's presence ('shadow' and 'trace' themselves being analogical predicates). Thus, the *analogia entis* is often associated with questions of truth, beauty and goodness – all areas where certain qualities in the world are regarded by natural theologians as being somehow inserted by God's creative will.

The attraction of this way of doing theology is that it is easy to see its ethical relevance: if being is the most meaningful analogue by which to speak of the world's creator, God, then responsibility towards all beings is of primary importance. This is the argument of a book like Sallie McFague's *The Body of God*, which makes some significant general claims about the right way to speak of God's relationship with the world. But 'body' theologies also have important things to say about such issues as the use of animals in research, women's right to abortion and IVF treatment – in fact, anything such that the theological language forms a strong link between God and the world. This is a major theme in contemporary theology, and should not be ignored.

Ultimately, most people are natural theologians to some degree; few of us would want to argue that God is utterly separated from the world. One such person, however, was Karl Barth, who argued that there is an infinite qualitative distinction between God and the world, as a consequence of the Fall, so that it is impossible to speak of God at all in human terms. The only way to speak of God, argued Barth, was by using God's own Word – Jesus Christ. This is the basis of Barth's understanding of the *analogia fidei*, the analogy of faith.

Stated simply, Barth thought that the answer to the question 'What is faith?' can only be: 'Jesus Christ'. Hence, the analogy of faith equals the analogy of Jesus Christ, which for Barth was the Incarnation. Theologians can speak of God by analogy, reasoned Barth, because God has spoken of God by analogy. Or, expressed another way: Jesus Christ is the language which God chose to speak to humanity. And since that language is simultaneously human and divine – remember the doctrine of the two natures – and therefore must look human, it cannot, by definition, simply attempt to describe God's being. God does not come to the world as God, argues Barth; God came as God *incarnate*, which also means as God concealed – hence the need to speak of God by analogy, because even after the Incarnation, God is not present in the world *as God*.

The *analogia fidei* is important, because it preserves the majesty and otherness of God, and as such it forms the basis of many impressive evangelical theologies. But it does so at the expense of relativizing the depth and significance of creation. The *analogia entis*, by contrast, speaks of the relationship between God and the world quite optimistically; but it does so at the expense of relativizing Jesus Christ. There is no easy way around this problem, and much of the theology which students will encounter becomes stuck upon how to reconcile the two. This difficulty is mitigated in practice, however, in so far as one uses *both* the *analogia entis and* the *analogia fidei* together; and indeed, it is hardly possible to separate them. Like so many things in theology, it is not a matter of either/or, but rather of both/and.

Focusing upon analogy in this way makes us realize that theology is really a way of reasoning and arguing, albeit interpretatively, and that, consequently, language is central to all the important concerns of Christian theology. Hence, it is logical that theologians can also employ other analogies to argue theologically. Examples are time, where past, present and future are used to speak of different qualities of God's relationship with the world; sexuality, where intimate personal relationships are predicated of the Persons of the Trinity; and art and culture, where, for example, notions of beauty and aesthetic intuition are taken as parallels to religious sensibility. As students will recognize, however, these can generally be regarded as alternative forms of the two basic analogies of being and faith. Thus, sexuality and art are themselves specific models of being; time is a specific question addressed to Christology; and so on.

All this is very attractive, and theologians occupy themselves for hours worrying about their language and analogies, vocabulary and grammar. But there is a far more fundamental question which confronts theologians: namely, the question of truth. In its Christian confessional form, this becomes the question of eschatology: are the things theology speaks of simply symbolic, or is there an independent divine reality which theology attempts to address? Do theological analogies signify something real, or are they simply nice stories which tell us something solely about ourselves?

Like it or not, theology must answer this question, and it is better done directly. My answer is as follows: yes, Christian theology speaks of something which it confesses to be independent and eschatologically real – namely, God. It knows about God through Jesus Christ, and therefore it speaks of God by analogy with faith. At the same time, it believes that the world is created through Jesus Christ, and therefore speaks of God by analogy with being. At all times, however, it claims that God is eternal, and that, consequently, there is an eschatologically real relationship between God and the world, which takes human form through the incarnation of the Son (in which time and eternity are united). This much Christian theology takes to be axiomatic. Failure to speak of God in these terms, or even failure to ask the question of truth in this way, is a failure of *Christian* theology.

The emphasis upon Christianity is important, and leads to the last of the classical problems which I want to discuss here: namely, Christianity's relationship with other religions. Historically, Christian theology has answered the question of truth by claiming sole possession of the correct answer: Christianity is true, and everything else is false. Given the qualities of pluralism and openness which I spoke of in Part I, however, such a bigoted answer will no longer do. Today, Christian theology must speak of the truth of other religions – but how? I think one can answer this question by concentrating on the confessional nature of religious truth, rather than on spurious attempts at objective verification. Or better: what we say is true is true, axiomatically; it allows of no demonstration. Thus, theologians should no longer speak of *the* truth, but solely of what is *true*; and what is true will depend upon the context in which the question is asked. Again, we return to the role of theology as interpretation, and try to make sufficient room to recognize the truthful qualities of religious traditions other than the Christian.

Why is such an attempt important? First, because it exemplifies the quality of humility, without which theology simply becomes hubris. Everything I have tried to say about interpretation, responsibility, analogy, the task of theology, militates against the false conviction that Christianity is simply 'the truth'. Second, because to close off the question of truth within just one corral, as so much Christian theology has attempted to do historically, is to limit God's revelation. Confessionally, Christian theology argues that God has been revealed through Jesus Christ. But confessionally it also acknowledges that this revelation was simultaneously a concealment. Thus, and equally confessionally, Christian theology cannot say that God's revelation cannot occur through other means and avenues; there is no viewpoint from which such an absolute negation could humanly be made. On the contrary, humanity's viewpoint is limited, because the Son appeared in limited form. At the very heart of Christianity, therefore, is room for incompleteness. And where there is such incompleteness, there is room for God to act through other means and avenues, including other religious traditions.

This is difficult for many Christians to accept, and it must be said that one does not often find such openness on the part of other religions towards Christianity. But it is fundamental to theology's contemporary situation, and is therefore something with which the student must wrestle. Classically, however, Christian theology was confronted by other situations.

3   Classical situations

The question of theology's classical situations is the question of theology's adaptability to the contexts in which it has been attempted, so it is an impossibly huge question to answer: every situation was classical to those who lived in it. At the same time, however, certain themes recurred frequently, and I want to look at these, albeit quite generally.

The classical doctrines and problems of theology were addressed by and large as part of Christian attempts at self-definition. And Christianity's need to define itself arose because it found itself in situations where it was addressed by the world at large, specifically with regard to its nature and right to exist. There is, then, a significant element of self-preservation in Christianity's attempts to deal with such recurring situations; such self-preservation is all about finding a place within a given world.

The world at large, however, did not address Christianity via endless generalities. Rather, it did so through quite specific questions and concerns. That is the way relationships normally proceed, of course: we do not speak to each other in generalities, but via specific ideas and by addressing specific issues. This is what happened to Christianity, so its theologies had to tackle the world at large on certain recognizable levels. Most importantly, those levels were liberation from power and oppression, secularism, philosophy, and the relationship between society and the individual.

Ironically, the relationship between theology and philosophy is the easiest to define, contrary to many preconceptions. Until this century philosophy was broadly sympathetic to theology, and theology drew heavily upon philosophy's languages and ideas for its own interpretations. An obvious example is Plato, who coined the word 'theology' in the first place; but there have been many others over the last 2,000 years and more. It is only in the twentieth century, with the advent of an aggressively assertive form of philosophy known as 'logical positivism', that theology has come under explicit attack. But today the situation is returning to that of earlier, more irenic times, particularly in the United States, where pragmatism's heritage always mitigated the worst excesses of logical analysis.

Logical positivism was an outcome of the age of Enlightenment, the privileging of reason since the seventeenth century. The age of Enlightenment was also the age of secularism, in which human existence within society and its institutions came to be explained without reference to God or another order of reality. From earlier discussion, one can see this development being characterized by modernity's attack upon eschatological realism – something which Christian theology had to repel. It was Barth's great contribution that he understood the danger of secularism's anti-eschatological stance, and resisted it throughout his career. Today this debate is still in full swing, particularly in the area of postmodernism, where important reflections upon the social character of language are affecting the way in which we understand talk about God's eternal reality, and God's presence in time in the world.

One of the great tenets of secularism, of course, is the notion of freedom, specifically freedom from outside interference. This question of freedom brings us directly to the relationship between the individual and society, wherein freedom finds its natural home in democracy and liberalism. Individual freedom translates in the modern world as independence, versus faith's notions of humanity's dependence upon God. At earlier stages in Christianity's development, the matter of dependence was not questioned. In the early Church, for example, non-Christians might argue about what people were dependent upon, rejecting God in Jesus Christ; but it never occurred to them that humanity might not be dependent upon anything. Similarly, Christianity's relationship to other religions in the Middle Ages was horrendously bloody, and Jews and Muslims fought bitterly with Christians in rejecting their religious imperialism. But Jews and Muslims never suggested that humanity was independent of God; quite the contrary.

All this leads to what is perhaps the sole recurring situation in which any theology, of any religion, finds itself: namely, that of liberation. Liberation from the world, liberation from God; liberation from oppression, liberation to oppress; liberation from society, liberation from the Church; liberation to be free in the world, liberation to be free in God: each of these illustrates the inherently transformative character of faith, whereby the constraints of this world are contrasted with the constraints/freedom of the Other. And in fact, this is what so much that is traditional and normative in the history of theology boils down to: the question of limit, of the sources of parameters determining both the way people practise their faith and the way in which they talk about it. It is the necessary tension between what people believe and the context in which they believe.

'Liberation' has become a key word in contemporary theology, and in the last chapter I want to talk about the work of theologians like Leonardo Boff and Jon Sobrino as examples of South and Central American liberation theologies. There we will see a very specific understanding of liberation. But here I want to end on a note of greater diversity.

It is impossible to say that theology, particularly as the interpretation of doctrine, was ever characterized by solely one, dominant situation; so, by focusing latterly upon the notion of liberation, I am not attempting to be prescriptive. Rather, I want to draw the student's attention to the necessarily tense relationship between doing and understanding theology. This tension is constitutive of theology's character, because theology, as no other discipline, wants to talk about both this world and that which is beyond. Whatever name one gives to the beyond – and Christian theology must name it Jesus Christ – there is always this fundamental tension. Previously it was played out against the background of an overwhelmingly theistic world; today this is being questioned as never before, both implicitly and explicitly. This is the world of contemporary theology, with which I want to end the book; for this is the world in which the student lives.

- Christian theology's classical doctrines shape its models by becoming recurring features. This is why they are classical doctrines, and why they are to be found – not always every one together, but always a good selection – in the vast majority of theologies. Their presence points towards a model being Christian.
- Classical problems recur because humanity remains recognizably familiar over the hitherto 2,000 years of Christianity. These problems are not prescriptive: theologies do not always consider them in this way or order. But the fact that they recur identifies them as significant for theology.
- Similarly, these classical situations are not exhaustive; but they are typical of the levels upon which theological activity occurs. They illustrate theology's need to address areas where people are in conflict with their situation and predicament, and thereby seek liberation.

10

Contemporary Issues

- Tension between issues and ideas in contemporary theology: the primacy of practice over theory, and its implications
- Reading the available literature: trends in theological publishing, the question of classic texts, approaching contemporary philosophy and social theory
- Future trends and developments: interfaith dialogue, sexuality, mass media and communication

One of the outstanding features of the Christian tradition has been its consistency; that, notwithstanding violence, persecutions and schisms, something recognizably Christian has persisted for nearly 2,000 years. It has supported a considerable variety of religious beliefs, some orthodox, some regarded as heretical. And it has generated a wide range of different academic disciplines to study the expression and communication of the Christian faith. Many introductory texts devote a great deal of space to this Christian history, and some attempt to elaborate the relationships between these different academic disciplines, such as biblical criticism and the philosophy of religion. The reality, however, is that studying theology today necessarily entails going beyond the relative safety of such existing parameters, to address the contemporary situation, which is dominated by one thing: social and cultural diversity.

In the previous chapter I discussed the doctrines which one could reasonably claim represented continuity in Christian theology, from the patristic period, through the medieval and Reformation eras, until modernity and the heart of the twentieth century. Doctrines such as the Trinity, Church, sacraments and the varied Christological ones – the Incarnation, cross, resurrection – have shaped and dominated the vast majority of theologies, so much so that even in the 1950s, two such conservative writers as Karl Barth and Rudolf Bultmann dictated the agenda of European theology. Even today, most higher education courses in modern theology focus on such figures, just as early Church history or doctrine courses focus on Irenaeus, Origen, the Cappadocians and Augustine. Such continuity is the cause of much repetition, and much comfort, for many students of theology.

Unfortunately for those who want this to continue, the diversity of contemporary theology is all pervasive, to the extent that it is no longer possible to speak of theology *per se*, but rather of theologies *per accidens* – or rather, theologies which originate in, and serve, their specific situation and constituency. As I have repeatedly argued in this book, this means that today's student must learn not just the material of subject areas, but rather specific skills, skills which are best described as interpretative. The preceding nine chapters have all been concerned with this general principle, just as they have all been designed to stimulate and develop the skills required by the successful student in this discipline.

All that remains is for the student to go away and practise these skills on specific problems and particular texts and ideas, be they biblical, as in New Testament criticism; or systematic, for example, the doctrine of the Trinity; interfaith dialogue, for example, the relationship between Christianity and Islam. In addition to encouraging students to apply these skills, I want to say something in this final chapter about what students will encounter as they undertake their work in the contemporary world. Without being too trite, this is *their* world, and, for all the many ways in which it is alienating, it is the context which they must render as intelligible as possible. In what follows, therefore, I want to offer some guidance as to the general terrain of contemporary theology, concentrating upon three specific questions: the dominance of issues over ideas, the exponential increase in theological literature, and likely trends in the future. Whilst acknowledging that different denominations will handle things differently, I want to argue that the themes I discuss will be central, whatever the denomination.

1 Issues or ideas?

To say that issues rather than ideas dominate contemporary theology is a little misleading – but only a little. What it really means is that contemporary theology is generally concerned with the practical situations in which it finds itself, rather than the conceptual apparatus necessary for such seemingly nebulous topics as 'cognition' or 'understanding'. Even more specifically, this emphasis is often characterized as *doing* theology rather than *studying* it. Certainly, that is the emphasis I find among students at the moment, something which manifests itself in a strong urge to write and argue about practical concerns. It is facile to rationalize this by speaking of a turn to radicalism in the 1960s or of an increasing politicization of people in the 1970s and 1980s. The simple fact is that the increase in awareness of cultural diversity, not just geographical but also social diversity, has found its way into academic theology – and not before time.

The causes of this are things which the majority of people in the Western world take for granted, so much so that they hardly pause to think about them: newspapers and magazines, TV and radio, jet travel and holidays abroad, daily encounters with foreign tourists, daily coverage of foreign governmental policy in the local and national media.

Consider the inauguration of Bill Clinton as President of the United States in 1992. Not only did Clinton make it clear that his wife, Hillary, was going to have an important role in the formulation of policy; he also invited Maya Angelou, the black poet and writer, to deliver the inauguration poem. These events signalled to the watching audience that both women's and black rights were going to be central to Clinton's presidency – something very important for the theologies concerned with these issues.

This story can be repeated with regard to Latin America and South-east Asia, where differing forms of liberation theology are flourishing. In Western Europe and North America, two developments predominate over all others: namely, feminist and womanist theologies and ecological ('green') theologies, reflecting these societies' concern with equality between the sexes and the welfare of the planet. The same things apply to these theologies as to the way in which we know and understand black theology in South Africa: great increases in the sophistication and scope of the media and communication have thoroughly transformed the way in which we understand our relationships to each other and the world, to the extent that we now relate the fate of the great whales to the way in which we understand God. Nor is this at all flippant: it is, after all, a theme in the Old Testament – read the book of Jonah – and an illustration of how the doctrine of creation is being interpreted.

Thus the character of theology has undergone a profound change since even the 1950s, and certainly since the pre-modern times which constitute much of the tradition and material students examine. And with this change, so too the way of studying theology has changed. If theology is no longer queen of the sciences, as it was in the time of Thomas Aquinas, for many it has become one social science amongst several others, so that today it shares an important affinity with such areas as social and cultural theory, language study, history and geography. Of course, it still has its own distinctive subject matter. But the significant question for today's student is not what is studied, but rather, how it is studied. The subject matter of Christian theology, after all, is recognizably familiar from the New Testament onwards. What change are the challenges faced in any given situation, such as the one in which the student finds him- or herself.

This is why I began this book by considering the relationship between theology and faith, and tried to show the way in which theological language and reflection are necessarily related to what people say and do in their belief and practice. Thus, theology is contextualized within faith, just as faith is contextualized within society and culture, history and geography. Demonstrating this fact is very simple: consider for a moment what a theologian would be ignoring if his or her interpretation of the doctrine of the Church (for example) failed to examine specific communities' relationships with groups other than Christian ones in their particular environment; if, say, one tried to write about the Church in occupied Palestine without considering Christian–Muslim relations and Palestinian–Israeli ones. Similarly, it would be impossible to write about the experiences of Christians in the United States without tackling the immense impact of race relations on that continent. The failings would be glaringly obvious – as, arguably, they have been in modern theology over the last 200 years.

Granted this situation, what can one expect of the student of theology? First, the qualities discussed in chapter 2 are of paramount importance. But second, and of equal significance, is the awareness necessary to see theological questions in their wider context. This is a requirement of any good education, encouraging the student to develop the openness required to think critically about an issue or idea by relating it to other issues and ideas. This leads naturally to a third expectation: namely, that students develop the ability to make connections between the issues and ideas they are studying, the context in which those ideas and issues were initially encountered/articulated, and the context in which the student is studying/interpreting. Good students make connections, in theology as in any other discipline. And when they make certain connections, they recognize others which were not apparent initially.

I want to illustrate this point by referring to three well-known examples, one in recent theology, one in systematic theology and one in ethics. First, I want to look at the reception of Dietrich Bonhoeffer's *Letters and Papers from Prison*, particularly the idea contained in the letter of 16 July 1944 to Eberhard Bethge, that 'God allows himself to be pushed out of the world onto the cross, and that is the only way that He saves us'.

In the late 1960s, 'death of God' theology interpreted this idea as if it were simply an objective claim by Bonhoeffer: namely, that God lets Godself be pushed out of the world, and therefore is dead. Thus, a very large metaphysical presupposition was brought to bear on Bonhoeffer's few words, by people with a very politicized agenda. In the process, however, two things vital to Bonhoeffer were ignored: first, that the idea in this passage needs to be understood within the context of Bonhoeffer's experiences of Nazism in general and his participation in the bomb plot to kill Hitler in particular; and second, Bonhoeffer's pervasive piety and spirituality, which is apparent throughout the text in question. Taken together, these two factors encourage the reader/student/theologian to understand Bonhoeffer's statement as an affirmation of a conservative doctrinal position – that God incarnate is pushed out of the world, on to the cross, thereby invoking both the Trinity and the Incarnation – within a situation of desperate social and religious crisis. What Bonhoeffer's words are *not* is precisely a metaphysical/cosmological rejection of Christian theism of the kind advocated by 'death of God' theology.

Similar points can be made about a recent treatment of a related systematic question: namely, the interpretation of the doctrine of the Trinity by Leonardo Boff in his book *Trinity and Society*. Boff reasons by analogy from the egalitarian, non-hierarchical relationships between the three Persons of the Trinity to the affirmation of such non-hierarchical relationships in all social, cultural and political situations. In the process, two important things are happening, one fairly obvious, the other much less so. First, Boff is making a deliberately provocative political statement: certain religious patterns can become the model for the way in which people as a whole live. Such an argument would hardly be treated seriously in Western Europe; but in Brazil Boff has a more receptive audience.

Second, however: where do those patterns originate? Or better, where does Boff's interpretation of the doctrine of the Trinity come from? The answer – from the story of Jesus of Nazareth and his relations with the Father and the Spirit – demonstrates the systematic complexity of Boff's position. His understanding of the Trinity is dependent upon his Christology, and his Christology is dependent upon a specific, materialist critique of the story of Jesus. The same critique underlies Boff's enquiries in other areas of systematic theology, such as the doctrines of Church and creation. This illustrates a general point, which is that, as soon as one starts looking for the connections which support a theological argument, more and more becomes apparent, in terms of both its applications and its foundations.

This point is reinforced if one considers the ethical issues surrounding the question of abortion, the right to life and a woman's right to control what happens to her own body. This is not a matter which can be resolved simply by citing facts and objective analysis, such as the foetus's apparent (and questioned) degree of independent existence at the age of, say, nineteen weeks. What we say should happen to the foetus is determined as much by our arguments and convictions about the integrity of the mother as a human being as by how we understand the sanctity of a life created by God. Similarly, the willingness of some people to kill others to prevent the death of a foetus is of profound theological importance – not least for the beliefs of those doing the killing.

These are three quite simple examples, and the connections they show are very straightforward; students will find far more complex ones fairly quickly. What I want to draw out, however, is the way in which the work of the theologian may involve detection, of the way in which an argument is uniquely communicated in a given situation, yet betrays clear relations to so much else that is occurring, both in theology and in other disciplines.

2   Reading the available literature

If all this sounds like a claim that the student should be able to detect a difference in the style and scope of more recent theological literature, this is true. Indeed, I can go even further, and argue without much fear of contradiction that the kind of book now being published differs quite radically from books of twenty-five to thirty years ago, and that the kind of books of even twenty years ago are no more. Being slightly facetious, one can say that big books on theology are becoming increasingly rare, and that the dictatorship of monumental tomes of dogmatic or systematic theology is well and truly ended. Although a systematic theologian myself, I cannot mourn the passing of texts like Karl Barth's *Church Dogmatics*; though the point of such relentless argumentation can still be asserted, thankfully its style has now passed into the hands of terser writers.

The *Church Dogmatics* is a useful example. Six million words in length, Barth's work amounts to a massive attempt to redescribe the subject matter of Christian dogmatics for his own

Reformed Church in the twentieth century. In that sense it is a contextual theology, but one with a big difference: namely, Barth's conviction, often unspoken, that Reformed dogmatics are *true* dogmatics. In this way the *Church Dogmatics* lays down an important marker, because it is still concerned with the question of truth *per se*; Barth still believes that one can speak of *the* truth as a quantifiable, though revealed, entity.

If one compares Barth's work with the series of books published by David Tracy over the last twenty years, however, particularly *Plurality and Ambiguity* (1988), the differences are striking. What Tracy is elaborating, with originality and verve, is an appreciably different way of looking at the problems of theology, one which takes seriously the developments of modernity and postmodernity, and offers a series of conclusions, sometimes contradicting earlier positions, which add up to a non-empirical, non-reductionist, non-objectivist interpretation of the way in which people live faithfully in the world. Of course, those books have taken Tracy beyond Christianity, and into explicit dialogue with other world religions. But that is not the point, the point is that Tracy is offering a methodology rather than an assimilable block of material. In this Tracy has done the student of theology a great service, because the kind of inquiry he or she should be undertaking is much closer to that of *Plurality and Ambiguity* than it is to that of *Church Dogmatics*.

What do I mean by this? That the essays which students of theology write today are much closer in style to Tracy than to Barth, and that this is important, given the specific context in which we now have to operate. For better or for worse, theology today is not the same as it was in the 1950s, and the questions, issues and ideas which must now be confronted are not those confronting Barth. As time has moved on, so theology's character has developed in line with Europe's changing culture.

This is good news for the student of theology, because it means that the books now being written have the same methodological concerns and constraints as those which impinge upon the student's own work. This is reflected by the ever-increasing range of issue-based books now being published, from liberation to ecological to feminist and womanist theologies, each of which, to varying degrees, demonstrates the qualities I discussed in chapter

2, being pluralistic, limited, applied, critical, creative and imaginative. Nowhere is this more apparent than in the work of David Tracy, which I want to consider briefly in greater detail. The text Tracy is best known for, and which is his major contribution to date to contemporary theology, is *The Analogical Imagination*, published in 1981.

Without going too deeply into its arguments, I can give the flavour of this work if I say that its title, *The Analogical Imagination*, tells us nearly everything we need to know about Tracy's agenda. Analogy, as we have seen, takes us directly into the world of traditional Christian theology in the best sense: it is reasoning from parallel cases, speaking about God on the basis of speaking about the world (and people), and as such is both intensely theoretical and intensely practical. Imagination is not something cognitive and subjective for Tracy, as it was for earlier theologians and philosophers, but is rather something social and cultural: it involves people and groups in communal activities, both recognized and unrecognized. It is, finally, something we do because of the situation in which we live, as people determined by our historical context, rather than as autonomous agents with the power to shape creation to our own wills.

From this last sentence we recognize something important about the way Tracy's argument wants to go. Tracy is not writing about something abstract called 'the Christian faith', but rather about what it is to be a member of a Christian community in an ambiguous, diverse, pluralistic world, one in which a certain degree of confusion, practical and conceptual, is the order of the day. Tracy acknowledges that we cannot escape from this confusion just because we want to. Rather, it is the context of our lives in the latter part of the twentieth century. Being true to our own world means being true to ourselves. And ultimately, it is this integrity which Tracy wants to urge upon everyone who thinks, reads, writes and communicates in the world today, whether a theologian or not.

At first sight disarmingly simple, Tracy's is in fact a complex, sophisticated position. It is founded upon an anthropology which is fast gaining a consensus in the academic world: namely, that humanity is to be understood not objectively, as 'stuff' which can be judged, measured and assimilated, but rather phenomenologically, by the language it uses to describe itself and its world. At bottom, Tracy argues that we are determined by the language we use to express ourselves, including all forms of visual and physical language, as well as the straightforwardly verbal. Indeed, many writers go even further, arguing that there is nothing other than language for people to understand and to give meaning – simply a realm of signs and symbols, metaphors and similes, which people engage to reason analogically about their own particular situation. Beyond language there might be another reality, God (for want of a better word); but as creatures in time we can only speak of this 'reality' as the axiom of a faith seeking understanding.

So the argument goes, although I would be surprised if everyone reading this book agreed completely with this position. After all, a central axiom of faith, as opposed to a theological one, seems to be that people refuse to question the truthfulness or reality of their own faith, with predictably dire consequences. But being a theology student today means moving beyond such a fideistic position, and embracing what commentators call the 'radical uncertainty' of the contemporary business of generating meaning in the world. Readers will come across words like 'postmodernism' and 'deconstruction', and perhaps be bewildered by them. But what such words signify is an acknowledgement that the interpretative questions we ask allow of no preset answers; that, finally, we are open to the experiences to which such questions lead us. There is no closure to theological questions in this world.

This is the attitude which David Tracy wants to encourage, and this is the attitude I think is necessary for today's theology student to develop in their work. Though Tracy is a Roman Catholic, these arguments are shared by many other theologians, from diverse Christian backgrounds. If one looks around at the best books being published at the moment and in the last few years, they are the ones which have forced us to think in this way, and to become open to the many voices which have been ignored and suppressed over the years of conformity in modern theology. But what about the voices that are likely to be heard in the next ten to fifteen years?

3　Future trends and developments

This is the final section of this book, and it is probably fair to say that it could prove to be the easiest to falsify. Identifying future trends and developments is notoriously difficult, in theology as in horse racing, and there is no guarantee that what I write here will be substantiated in the coming years. That said, however, and restricting myself to the world of academic theology rather than the world of Church and faith, where very different debates may well ensue, I want to discuss three things which I believe will become increasingly significant: interfaith dialogue, sexuality and the mass media. As I have indicated, these are my concerns, those of a liberal-catholic Anglican. But they will be shared by at least some members of most denominations in the Western world.

My comments about openness and radical uncertainty should have made the reader think about religions other than Christianity: their claims to truth and the way in which Christian theologians relate and respond to their arguments and beliefs. This is particularly relevant in the Western world, both in Europe and in North America, where we are surrounded by widespread cultural diversity, including religious diversity, and where there is no longer any excuse not to engage with a wide range of religious traditions. If, as some maintain, we are entering a post-Christian era in these parts of the world, where the dominant culture of the preceding thousand years is finally yet rapidly declining, then there are many new encounters and experiences to fill the void. Theologians like John Hick and David Tracy, though of differing generations, are attempting to push Christian theology towards a deeper engagement with interreligious dialogue, justifying this step primarily by the methodological considerations which we have been discussing throughout this chapter.

The situation is a fluid one, as teachers of theology and religious studies are drawn further into questions of interfaith dialogue. The same can be said for the second area I want to discuss in this section, the relationship between theology and sexuality, where by 'sexuality' I refer to both a general anthropological principle – a quality integral to being human, rather than simply being male or female – and gender-specific behaviour. Both are matters which students will encounter in modern theology courses, with reference to feminist and womanist theologies, and in courses of ethics, thereby illustrating this chapter's argument regarding the practical nature of the discipline today.

If I begin my discussion by quoting two recent examples from the Church of England, it is solely to demonstrate how contemporary theology is more advanced than many ecclesial establishments. The two items are, first, the Bishops' Report of 1992 on sexuality and second, the decision in 1992 to permit the ordination of women as priests. The former in effect condemned homosexual love, if active, as deviant and un-Christian; the latter, though a majority one continues to cause great distress within the Church of England as opposition becomes increasingly entrenched. Both cases were characterized by two factors: considerable theological ambiguity and almost total divorce from developments in the world of professional theology.

What do I mean by this claim? I mean that the overwhelming consensus in contemporary theology is that questions of sexuality can no longer be addressed by reference to a *de facto* code or 'Law', whereby certain beliefs or (more generally) practices are condemned and rejected in favour of the apparently normative conduct of the majority. Rather, questions of sexuality are now understood as matters of social and cultural reference, which means as ones referring to the created nature of humanity in the world. Thus, humanity's creatureliness finds expression in a wide variety of ways, just as humanity's ability to love finds expression in a variety of ways, and just as God's love for humanity finds expression in a variety of ways – one of the most important being compassion and support. One can recognize, therefore, what is happening: theology's increasing awareness of the complexity of what it is, socially and culturally, to live in the world is informing theology's understanding of what it is to be human in a wide variety of ways and situations. What is happening today is that this awareness is being directed towards questions of sexuality, with predictably pluralistic results. That this is happening in the United States, as well as in Europe, is illustrated by contemporary debates within the Republican party, nurtured by Newt Gingrich and others, concerning the identity, constitution and ideology of 'family values' – with potentially legislative implications.

The important thing to bear in mind here, I think, is the process of dismantling and construction which theology is currently witnessing, the way in which existing prejudices, based upon a monolithic view of humanity, are being broken down and left behind, and are being replaced by a much more progressive understanding of humanity and its relationship to God. As already stated, students will find this attitude in many books on feminist and womanist theologies, as well as many books on ethics. But most importantly, they will find it developed in the world of contemporary media and communication, which is fast becoming a dominant concern for the character of theology in Europe and the United States.

The juxtaposition of sexuality and the media is a happy one at this point, because it is obviously via such mass market publications as *The Sun* in Britain and *The National Enquirer* in the United States that the issues of sexual behaviour and, as importantly, people's perceptions and prejudices regarding sexual behaviour, become ever more discussed and assimilated within popular culture. This is true both in a general sense – consider the scandal surrounding Bill Clinton's sexual encounter with Monica Lewinsky – and more specifically in religious matters: 'Priest Seduces Parishioner' and variants thereof are popular favourites of bored desk editors on a slow newsday. While we may be appalled by the language and the invasion of privacy, we are steadily becoming more and more used to the infiltration by the mass media of the areas of sexuality and religion and theology.

For today's student, asking whether this is a good or a bad thing is no longer a relevant question. What is relevant is that it is a *fait accompli*, and that, consequently, theology as a form of public discourse, albeit one in which comparatively few people participate, is now functioning in large part under new rules and guidelines. More pertinently, what I mean is that theology today is both more liberated, in the sense that it is no longer controlled by obsolete norms and opinions, and yet, paradoxically, more accountable to a wider and cooler audience. That audience stretches as far as the potential of mass communication media – radio, newspapers, pre-eminently television, the Internet – which, as recent history in the United States demonstrates, is enormous:

witness the power and influence of television evangelism, with an ability to create instant wealth unparalleled in theology and religion since the sixteenth-century conquistadors in Latin America – and, some would add, with as little morality.

What is most interesting about this development in contemporary theology is the manner in which it is calling people to communicate theologically in ways for which they have not been trained and in situations in which they often feel distinctly uncomfortable and alienated. We all have our favourite image of the absent-minded professor, dragged off the street by local television to address the nation on a matter of vital importance to the state. Well, it happens in theology and religion, and it often has comical results. But what is beginning to happen is that people are acquiring the ability to perform well on television, thereby stimulating considerable interest from a hitherto undreamt-of audience. That television evangelists and major politicians can now influence the way in which people understand and express their religious beliefs, simply by being skilled communicators and visual presenters, may not be an entirely new fact of life. But it is one which should give every student considerable pause for thought as he or she learns how this discipline works.

- Much pressure in contemporary theology turns attention towards practice and away from theory; but issues need ideas if they are to be addressed meaningfully and positively.
- Contemporary books illustrate this tension, both good and bad. In reading theology, therefore, students must constantly test the arguments presented to them: that is their purpose!
- Future trends and developments will continue theology's movement towards the progressive (see chapter 2) – hence the consideration of interfaith dialogue, sexuality, and mass media and communication. Each will test theology's ability to reflect its basic qualities over the next twenty years.

Conclusion: The
Ever-widening Ripple

One adage people are taught when they start writing things, perhaps at school but certainly by the time they reach higher education, is not to include any new material in conclusions. Chapters are for new material; conclusions are for summaries, goals and, well, ... conclusions. So: what conclusions can we draw from this introduction to the study of theology?

First, and despite everything I have said about the novelty of developments in contemporary theology, I hope students are reassured by the familiarity of much of what they have read. A significant feature of faith, as I stressed in chapter 1, is its normality: so many people are faithful; so many faithful actions and themes are intelligible simply by reference to our daily lives. One of the most important qualities which students of theology need to develop, therefore, is the ability to be flexible, to adapt to the different constraints of different situations, to understand the sheer variety of religious belief, practice, custom and experience. I described such flexibility in chapter 2, in straightforward terms: as pluralistic, limited, applied, critical, creative, imaginative.

Second, however – and allaying the anxieties caused to many by a call for flexibility – theology today, as it always has been, is undertaken within certain recognizable parameters. Whatever the circumstances under which people attempt to speak of God in Jesus Christ, and however one understands the truth of their statements, *Christian* theology takes place according to identifiable principles and in terms of acknowledged resources. I spoke of these resources as responsibilities in chapters 3–6, on language and experience, the Bible, history and tradition, and society and culture. And I emphasized in those chapters the accumulated knowledge and understanding which Christian theology has gained through its practitioners. Theology is an open discipline, certainly. But it is one informed by nearly 2,000 years of *theolo-*

gians of all descriptions, people who have contributed to the way in which we today understand the ground upon which we build theological models. It sounds romantic; in one sense, it *is* romantic. But it is also an incontrovertible fact: students today follow those who have gone before, leaving traces in the dust.

The ability to practise theology, consequently – my third point – to appreciate its shape as doctrine and to pursue its task as interpretation, is an informed ability: it takes place in a context of reading and discussion of other people's theological models and ideas. The excellence with which one practises theology is directly related to the energy one expends upon reading and discussion, allied to the related disciplines of thinking and writing. Simply to be able to utter one's own thoughts about God does not make one a theologian. Together with that ability, another is required: that of being able to listen to, interpret and learn from, others' models. Early in the book I called for humility, and I want to reassert now that humility is essential to any developed understanding of doctrine and its interpretation. It is part of the preparation required before one can speak *analogically* of God.

This necessity is illustrated, fourth, in the recurring themes and contemporary developments of Christian theology, be it the doctrine of the cross, fundamental to everything theologians might want to say, or coconut theology from the Pacific Islands. Despite the fact that throughout this book I have deliberately emphasized theology's kinship with other social sciences – those attempts to understand how humanity lives – it must not be forgotten that theology's final goal and object are qualitatively different from those of any other science: to speak of *God*. Whatever one's own beliefs, theistic or otherwise, one should recognize the aspirations with which humanity speaks of that which it believes to be beyond its knowledge and understanding. Even this much makes theology special.

If this sounds too daunting, then readers should be reassured: the ability to think and write theologically is a learned skill, a discipline which takes time to master. To this end the chapters of this book have been deliberately short and succinct, their introductions and summaries as limited as ambition allowed. The Glossary is there to be used, and will answer the student's immediate questions about terminology whilst leading them towards new ones. That need is also addressed by the Suggestions for Further Reading, which I have likewise kept short, selecting only those texts which I believe will aid the first-year student just setting out. No one expects students to read every item on such a list. But it is there to be used. It, too, is simply a tool, as effective as the student makes it.

Such utilitarianism neatly encapsulates my approach to writing this introduction to the study of theology. It is not intended to be a textbook like some, which include every bit of information normative for a specific religious position, or a source of objective knowledge, but rather a stimulus to exercise. I firmly believe that the task of the lecturer or teacher is to encourage the development of the ability to think theologically. It is comparatively easy to provide information culled from other sources, themselves culled ultimately from other sources, and so on, *ad infinitum*. It is another thing to help someone acquire a new skill.

Finally, I used the expression 'ever-widening ripple' in my text, and have reintroduced it here as the title of my conclusion. By its use I want to encourage students to understand their own activity within the wider context of an ever-expanding number of people who engage in Christian theology, who have traditionally interpreted doctrine to produce new models and new doctrines. Some people prefer the simile of a journey, likening theology to the movement and progression of travel. But if we think of the waves which envelop us as we swim in the sea, then I believe we come closer to the reality of what it is to study theology. Theology has no absolute limits; it expands, like water, to fill a given space. And as it expands, so it encompasses those who share its languages and qualities. One must learn to adapt to this situation.

Glossary

Apophatic/Kataphatic 'Apophatic' is a term used to describe the impossibility of speaking of God; hence the apophatic tradition emphasizes this impossibility. 'Kataphatic' is used to characterize the argument that one can speak of God because God has spoken God's Word – hence the kataphatic tradition draws heavily on the language of Christology. 'Apophatic' and 'kataphatic' are often used in theology to speak of God's absence and presence, respectively.

Axiom A principle which allows of no demonstration. In Christian belief, for example, it is axiomatic that God was in Christ.

Catechism A form of training organized by the Church, proceeding via question and answer, in which new believers are instructed in the doctrines of the Christian faith.

Creeds Statements (effectively, lists of key beliefs) of Christian doctrine, agreed ecumenically by churches in the early history of Christianity, which are confessed by believers as summaries of the faith. The Nicene and Apostles' Creeds are often spoken aloud in the liturgy of the Word.

Dialectic Mode of argument in which a proposition or hypothesis is then opposed by a counter-proposition or antithesis, leading to a conclusion or synthesis. A major style of theological argument in the medieval Church, perhaps best typified in Thomas Aquinas's *Summa Theologiae*.

Economic/Immanent In theology, 'economic' is used to describe God's revelation of Godself in the world, specifically through the Word, Jesus Christ. 'Immanent' is used to describe

God's being in and of itself. Since this is not objectively possible, talk of God's immanent being is analogical. The contrast between the two is usually made by saying that theology speaks of God's immanent being in terms of God's economic revelation in Jesus Christ.

Ecumenism Movement or attitude directed towards the worldwide unity of Christianity, as witnessed today in the proclamations of the World Council of Churches. Derived from a Greek word meaning 'the inhabited world'.

Empiricism Science based on observation or experiment, not theory, regarding sense-data alone as valid information.

The Enlightenment The 'Age of Reason', from the mid-seventeenth century onwards, which established the modern world on the principles of rationality and civil society.

Epistemology Theory of knowledge, addressing the question, 'What good reasons do we have for what we think we know?'

Eschatology A form of apocalyptic, 'seeing the heavenly secrets', eschatology is the Christian doctrine of the end of the world and its associated Last Judgement. More generally, eschatological language is used to describe the relationship between time and eternity, particularly in modern theology.

Hermeneutics The theory of interpretation, taking account of the historical and social context of both text and reader. In modern hermeneutic theory, the meaning of a text is generated by an engagement between two such contexts, so meaning is historical, not inherent to the text itself. Hermeneutics is contested by those who argue that it is possible to state objectively what the meaning of a text is.

Liberalism Progressive development in modern political and social thought, which has found its way into theology. It argues for individual freedom and advocates reason as the principal quality of knowledge and understanding. Liberal theologies acknowledge the influence of society upon Christian belief, often in the form of reason, alongside the Bible and tradition.

Liturgy Liturgies are formalized rituals which normally take place in churches, in which believers come together to worship God and celebrate their faith. Examples are the liturgy of the Word – the reading of the Bible and teaching (the sermon) – and the liturgy of the Eucharist, or the celebratory remembrance of Christ's Last Supper.

Metaphor A trope or literary form whereby a name or expression is applied to an action or object to which it is imaginatively but not literally applicable. For example, 'The moon's a balloon', or in theology, 'God is love'.

Metaphysics A category of philosophy concerned with different forms of enquiry into being and knowledge. Thus, ontology (being) and epistemology (knowledge) are both forms of metaphysical thinking.

Orthodoxy/Heresy Simply understood, the distinction between authorized and condemned teaching in Christianity (a distinction identified and exercised by the teaching authorities of the Church).

Paradox Apparently self-contradictory statement or belief which contains a higher truth. Theology speaks of the paradox of the Incarnation, whereby God becomes human – that is, that which is not God.

Pluralism In religion and theology, a recognition of different valid ways of speaking of and believing in God. Often used to describe acceptance of different world religions as equally valid and meaningful. In contemporary theology, used to describe the argument that different contexts will generate different theologies.

Sacrament 'An outward and visible sign of inward, invisible grace', according to popular devotion, a sacrament is a vehicle, sanctioned historically and traditionally by the Church whereby grace – the presence of God – is mediated to believers. In Roman Catholicism there are seven sacraments: baptism, confirmation, Eucharist, marriage, holy orders, penance, holy unction. Protestant churches recognize only baptism and Eucharist.

Symbol   Something which by common agreement demonstrates the qualities of an idea, action or being by analogy or approximate characterization. More forcefully, some argue that symbols are indicative of deeper realities which impinge upon human existence. Others argue that they are solely linguistic constructs.

Theism   A term used to describe the general argument that God exists, and thereby the set of presuppositions about the possibility of speaking of God with which theology operates. Its opposite – atheism, the rejection of belief in God – helps to define it further.

Suggestions for Further Reading

The aim of an introduction to theology is not to make people read endless pages of facts and interpretation, but rather to foster the skills and confidence required to think theologically. To that end, I have listed solely those titles which I think will help to open up the issues and questions which I have discussed in the book, without burdening students with too much background information. Those who simply require knowledge will be able to find it in the major encyclopedias and textbooks.

Leonardo Boff, *Trinity and Society*. New York, 1984.

Walter Brueggemann, *The Bible and Postmodern Imagination*. London, 1993.

Avery Dulles, *The Craft of Theology: From Symbol to System*. Dublin, 1992.

Francis Schüssler Fiorenza and John P. Galvin (eds), *Systematic Theology: Roman Catholic Perspectives*. Dublin, 1992 (especially pp. 1–87).

Stanley Hauerwas, *Dispatches from the Front: Theological Engagements with the Secular*. Durham, NC, 1994.

Walter Kasper, *Theology and Church*. London, 1989.

Fergus Kerr, *Theology after Wittgenstein*, 2nd edition. London, 1997.

George Lindbeck, *The Nature of Doctrine*. London, 1984.

Sallie McFague, *The Body of God: An Ecological Theology*. London, 1993.

Alister McGrath, *Christian Theology: An Introduction*. Oxford, 1994.

William Placher, *Unapologetic Theology: A Christian Voice in a Pluralistic Conversation*. Louisville, Ky, 1989.

Heikki Räisänen, *Beyond New Testament Theology: A Story and a Programme*. London, 1990.

Dorothee Sölle, *Thinking about God: An Introduction to Theology*. London, 1990.

David Tracy, *The Analogical Imaginations*. London, 1981.

David Tracy, *Plurality and Ambiguity*. London, 1988.

Frances Young, *The Making of the Creeds*. London, 1991.

Index